The Illustrated
WINESPEAK

The Illustrated

WINESPEAK

RONALD SEARLE's

wicked world
of
winetasting

SOUVENIR PRESS

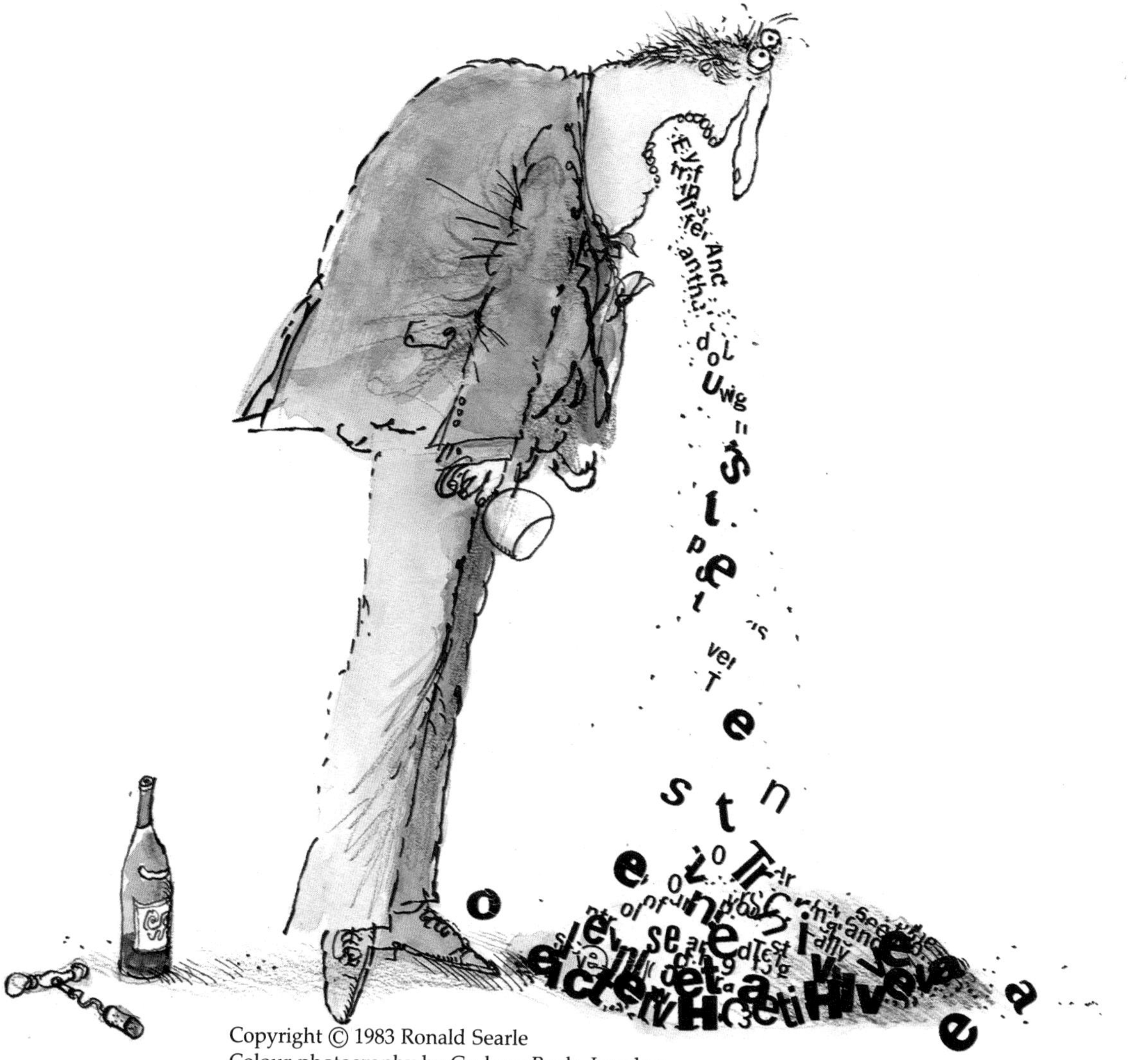

Colour photography by Graham Bush, London
First published 1983 by Souvenir Press Ltd,
43 Great Russell Street, London WC1B 3PA
Reprinted 1984 (twice)
Reprinted 1985 (twice)
Reprinted 1986, 1987

ISBN 0 285 62592 6

Printed in Great Britain by
Hazell Watson & Viney Limited,
Member of the BPCC Group,
Aylesbury, Bucks

The tortuous phrases that are frequently used when trying to describe music, fade into insignificance beside the agonising and often excruciating acrobatics of those whose duty it is to enlighten the baffled consumer regarding the more esoteric aspects of, say, Rotterdam rouge.

The art of wine-tasting has its own band of remarkable poets, those whose words vividly conjure up unimagined nuances and have us panting to experience the excitement and glow of drinking a particular bottle. Alas, they are as rare as the greatest vintages of the wines that dutifully pass their lips for our benefit.

The rest, that grotesque international band of snobbish inarticulate sponges, who are incapable of thinking beyond their incestuous little circles, do as much harm to the world of wine as they do to the language. Their day will come . . .

All the phrases in this little book have been plucked from unacknowledged but absolutely authentic sources. You could do worse than ponder over some of them. Cheers!

R.S.

Delightful bouquet

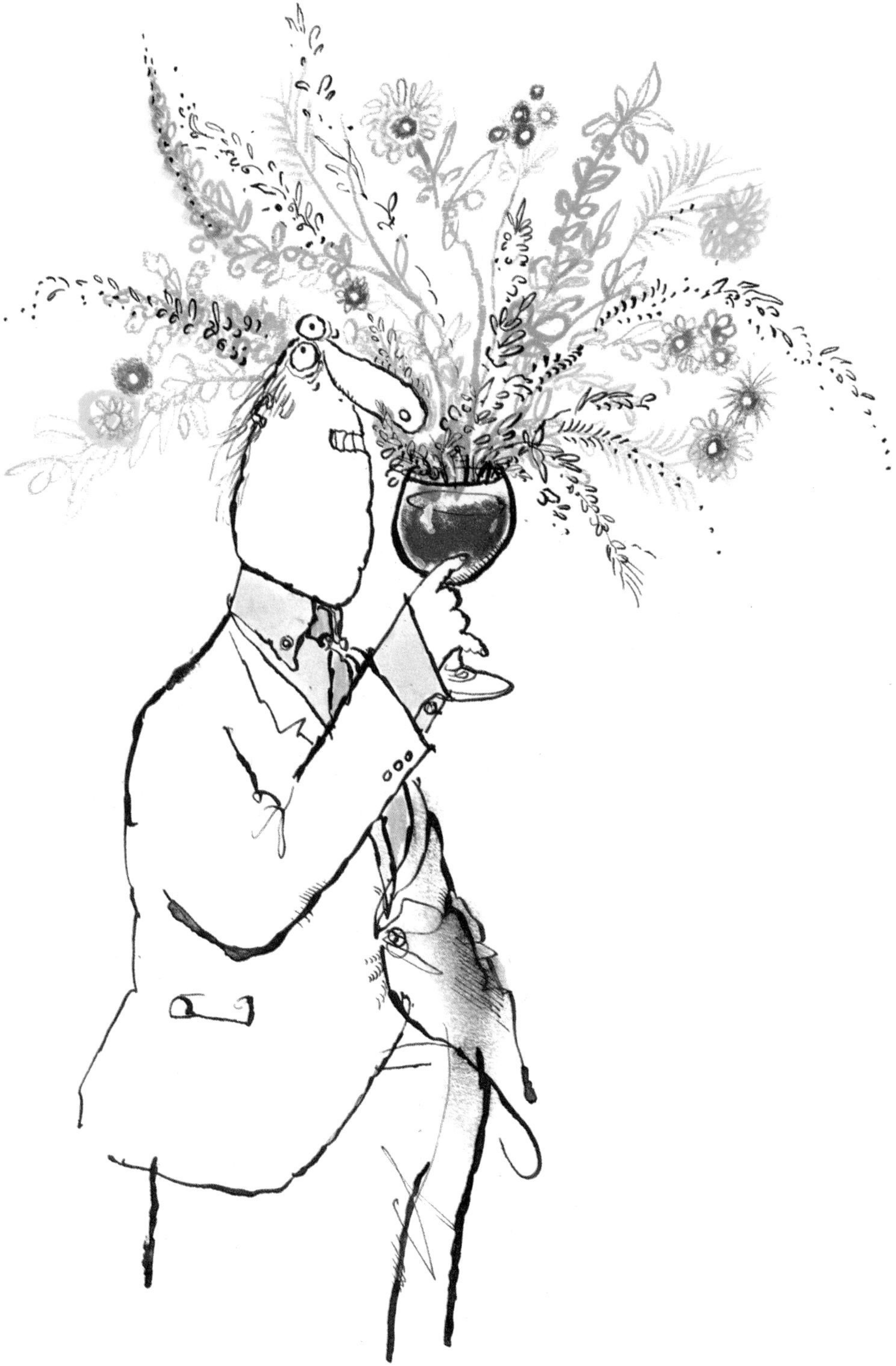

Gay and sprightly

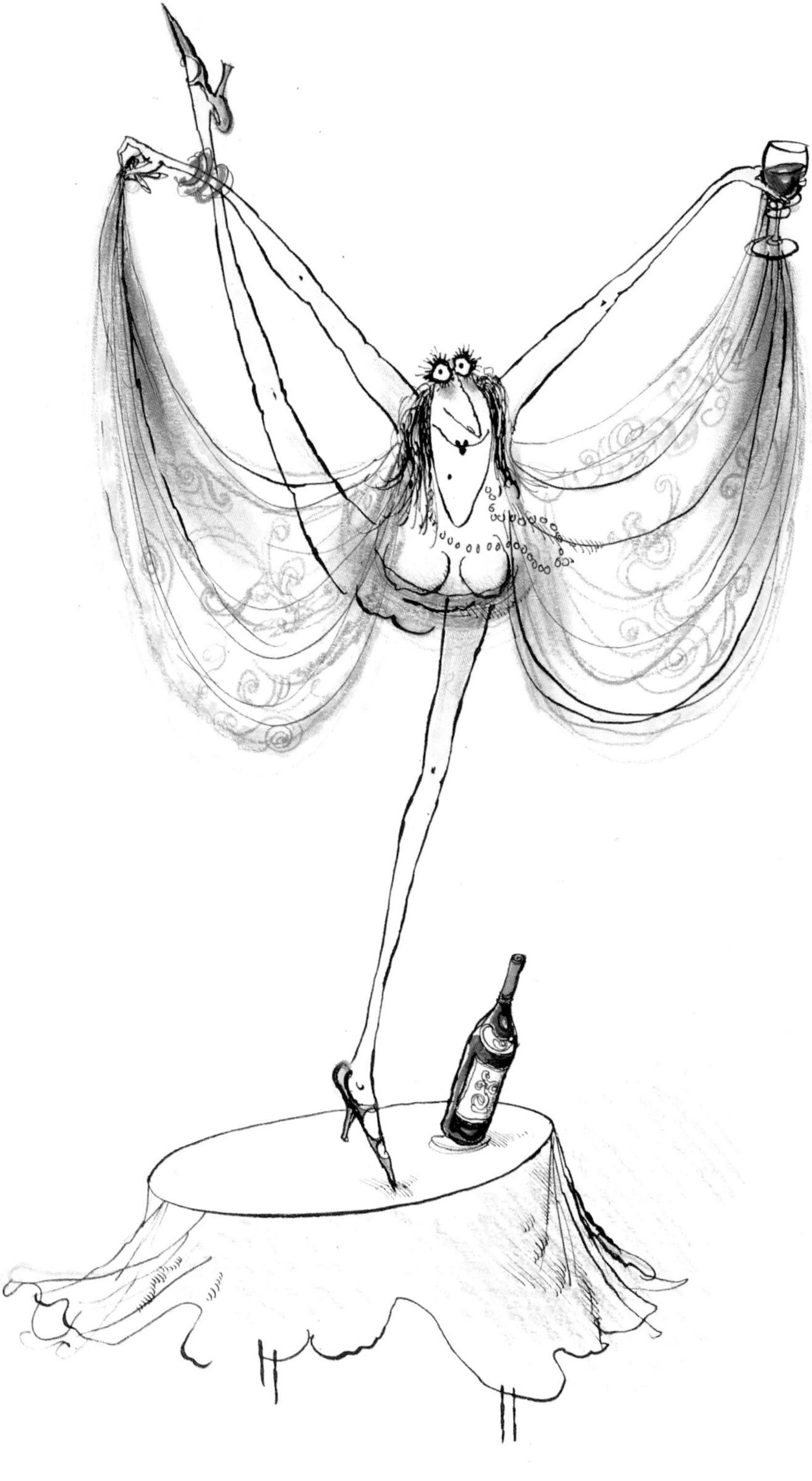

Distinctive nose

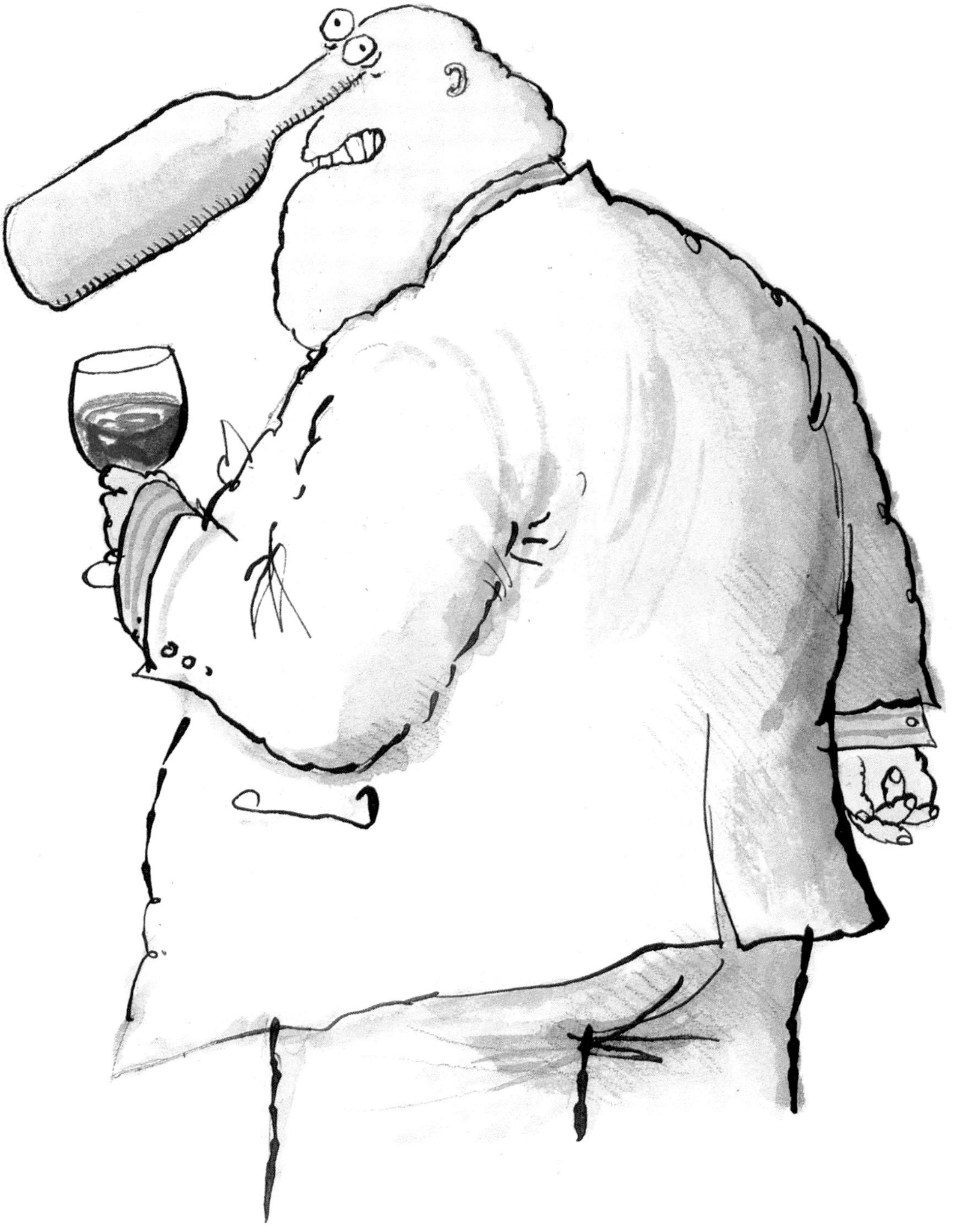

Subtle and of great richness

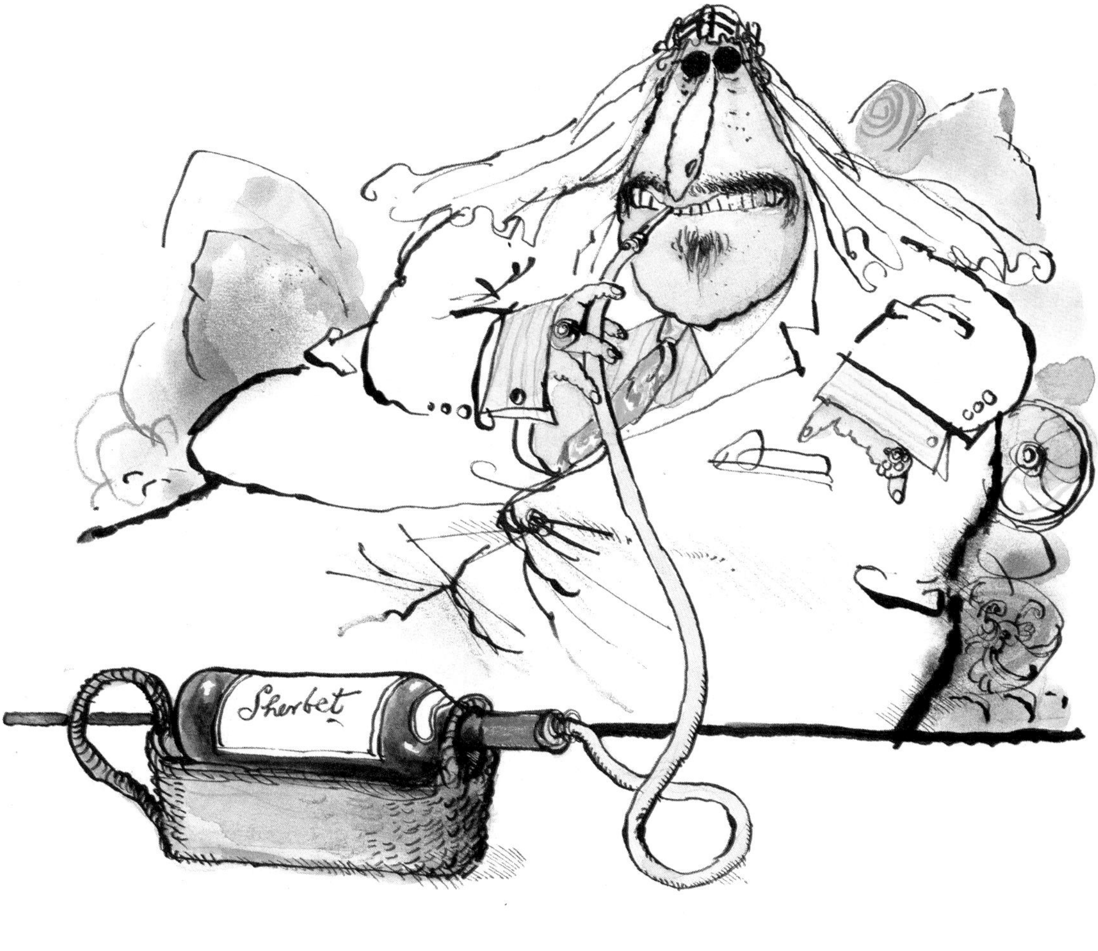
Sherbet

Intense, aromatic, lots of body

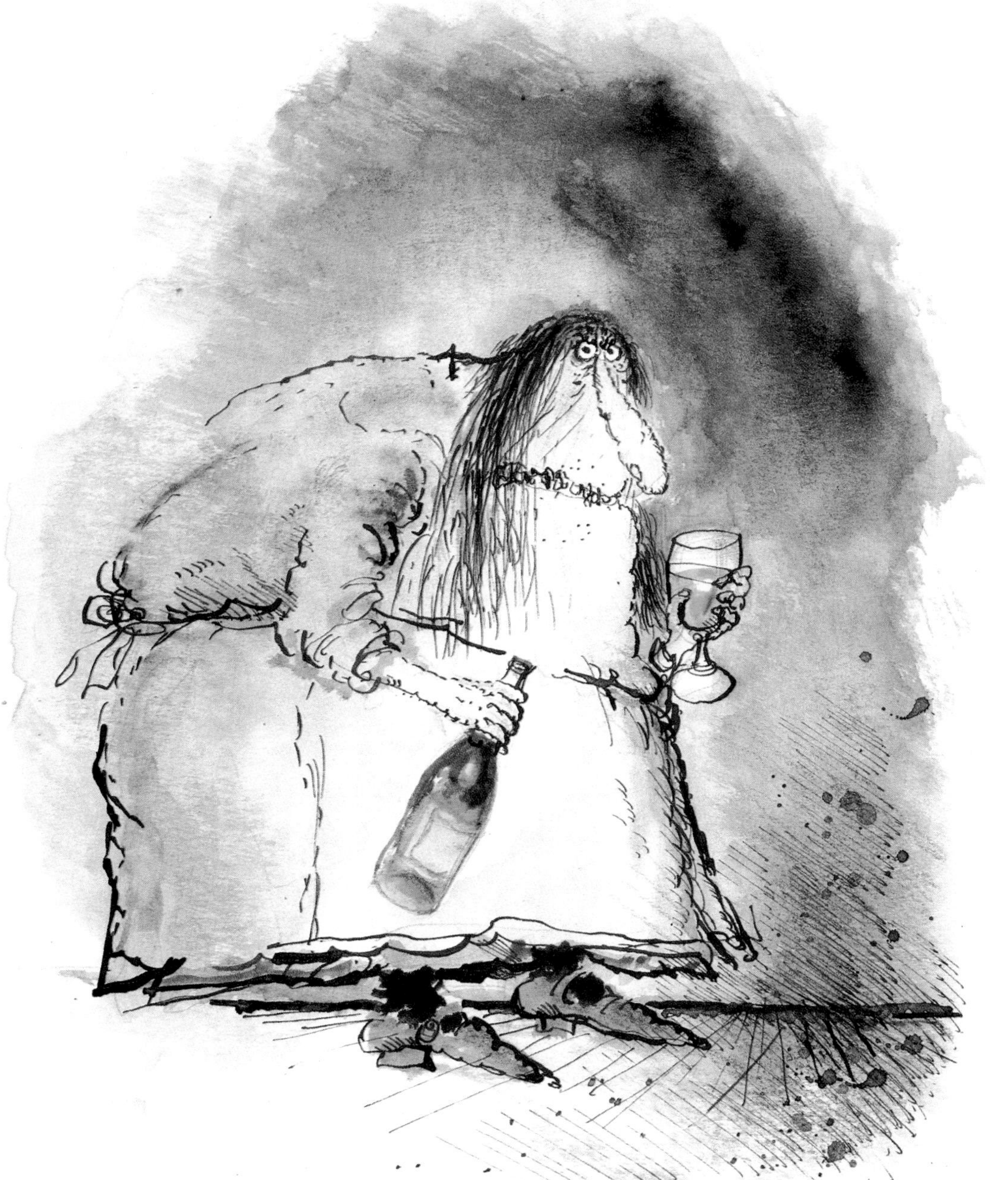

Unusual

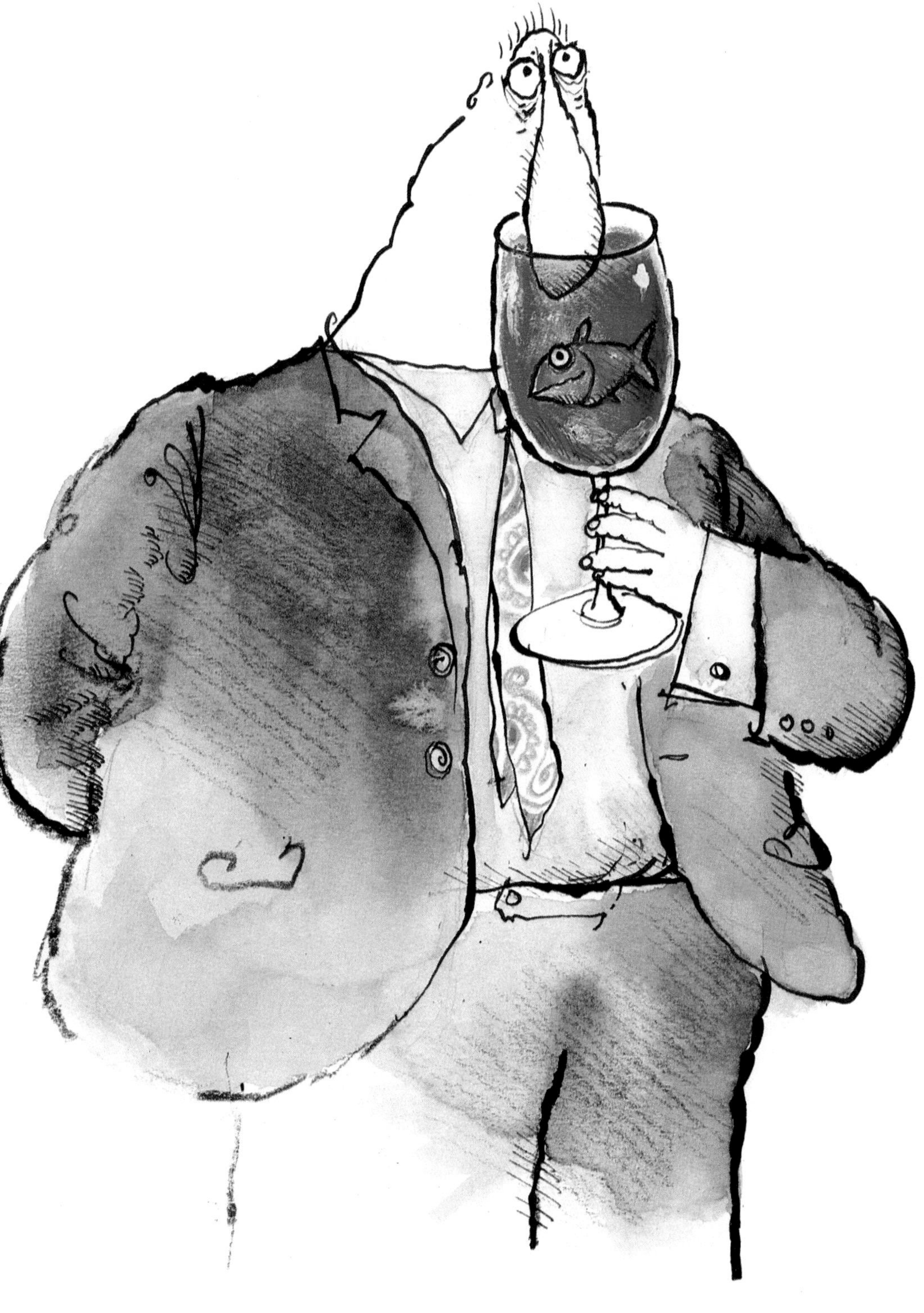

Pleasantly scented, very agreeable

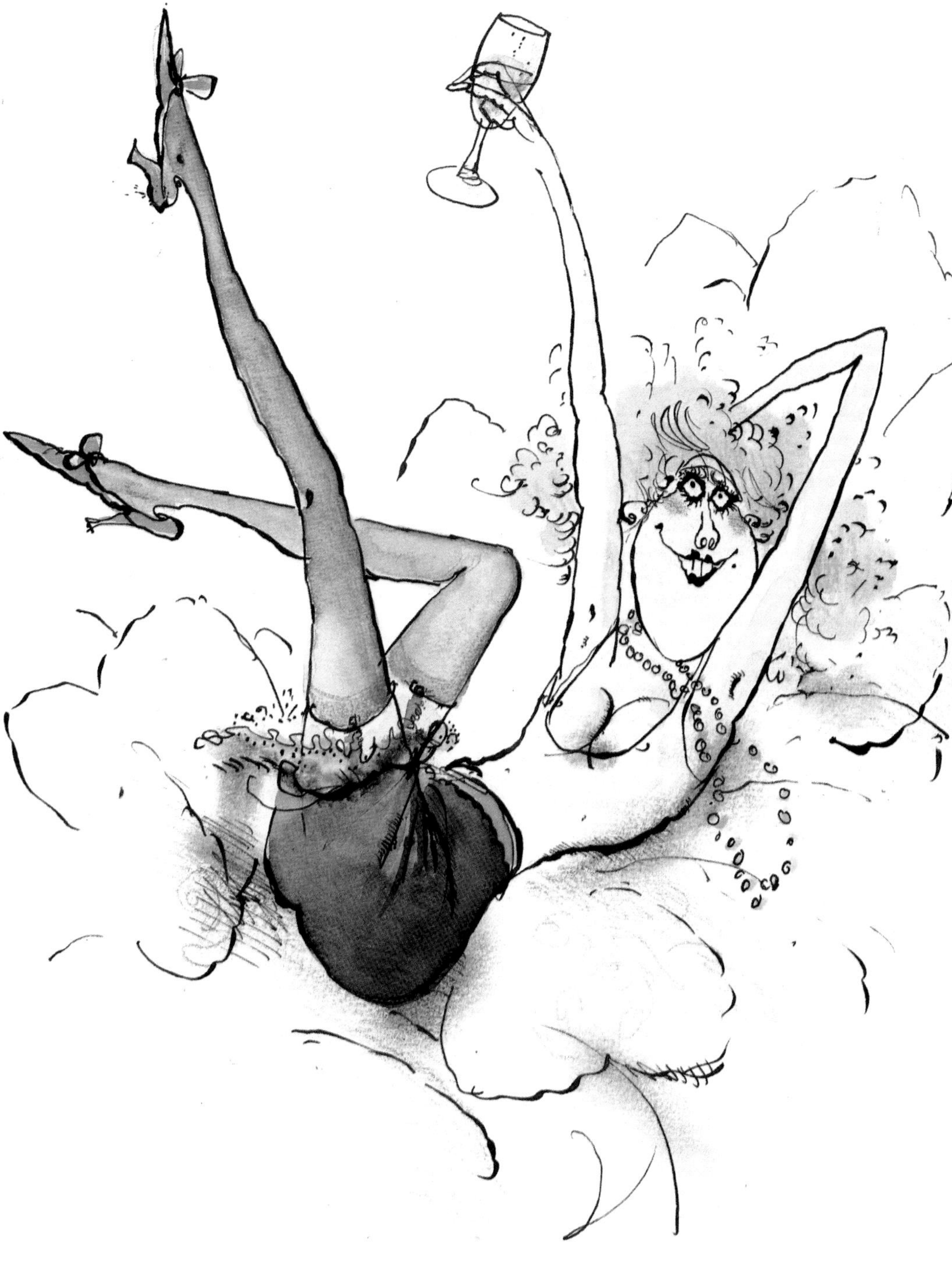

Unpretentious

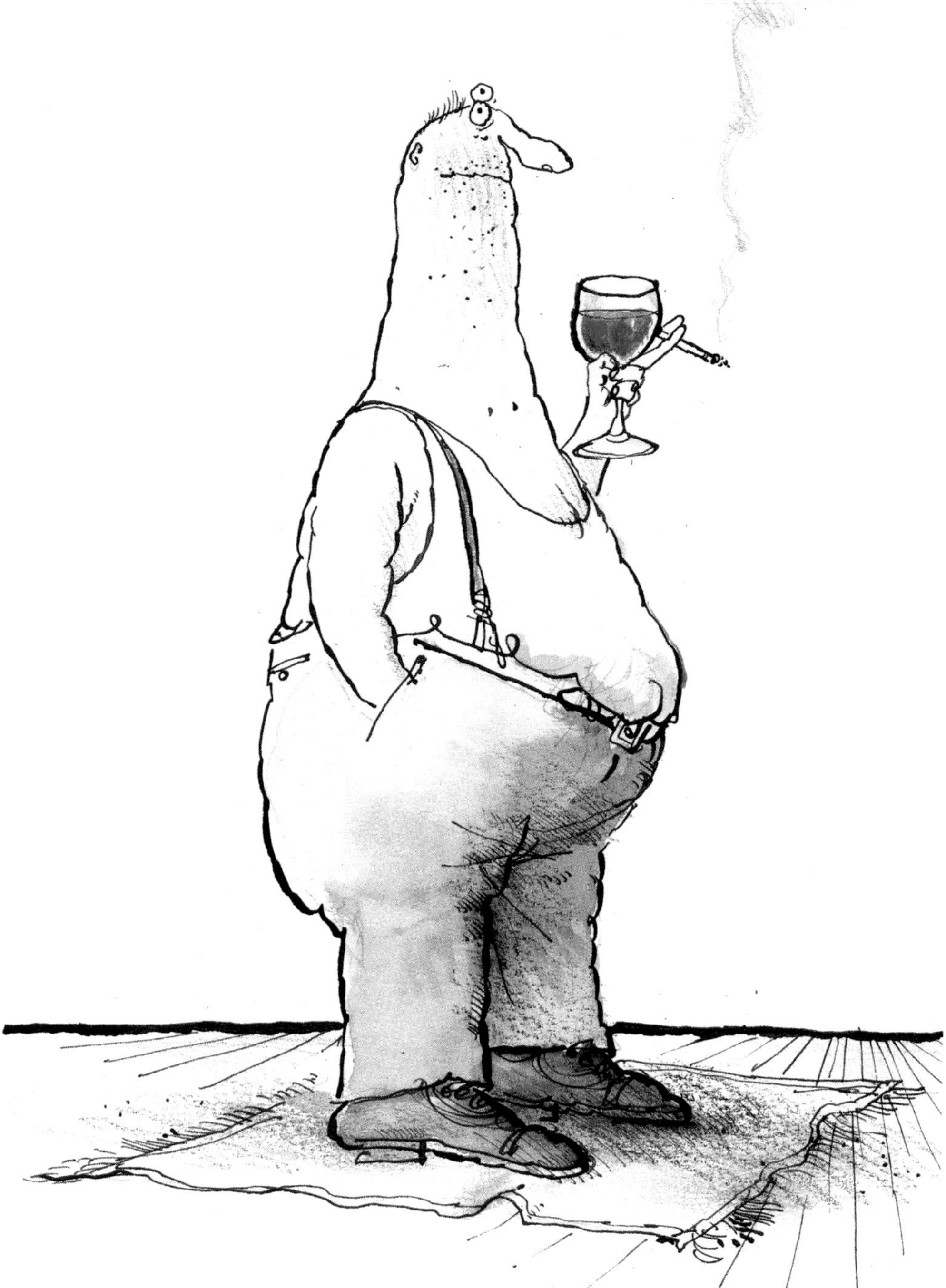

Notable in its category

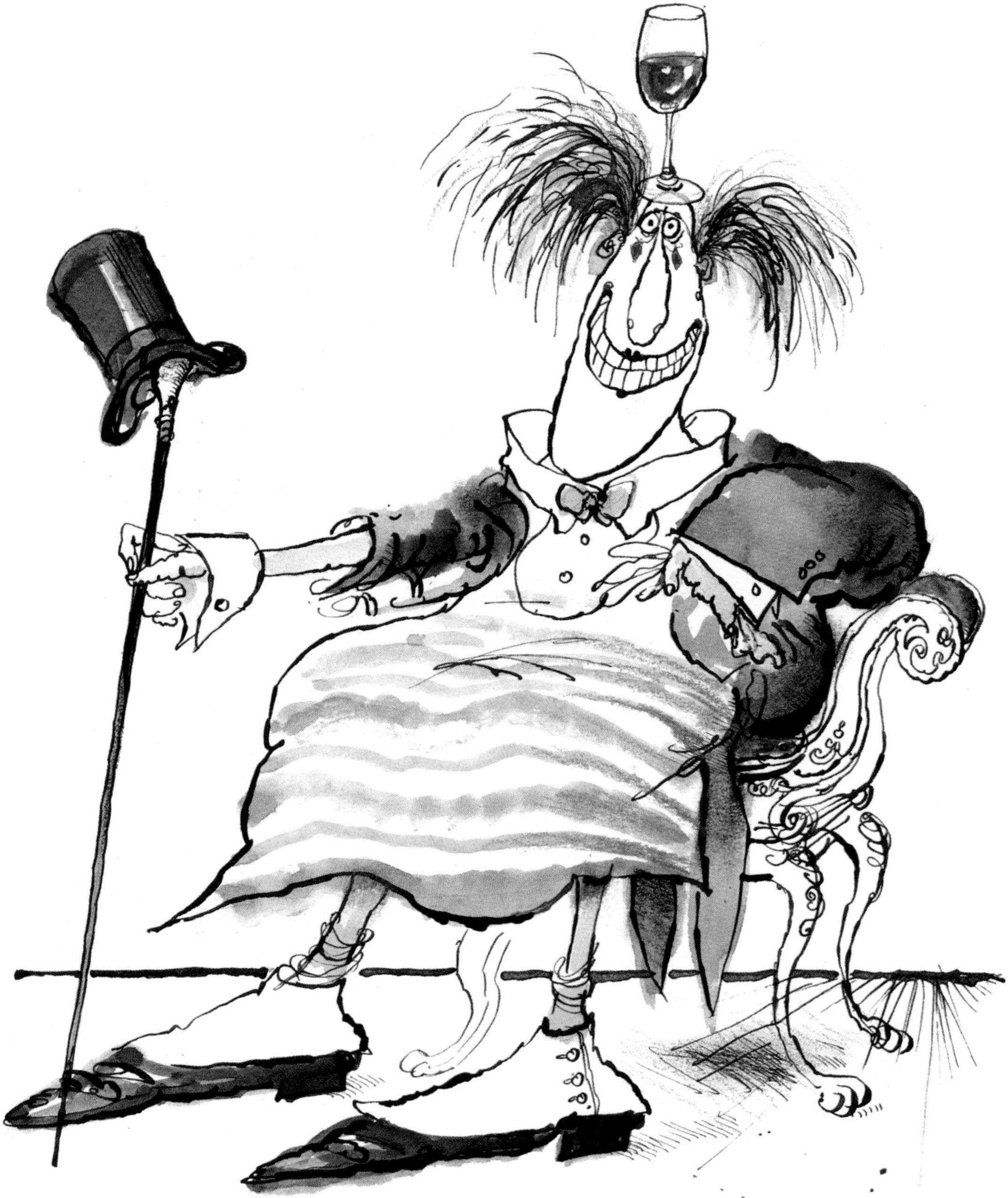

Exceptionally full-bodied

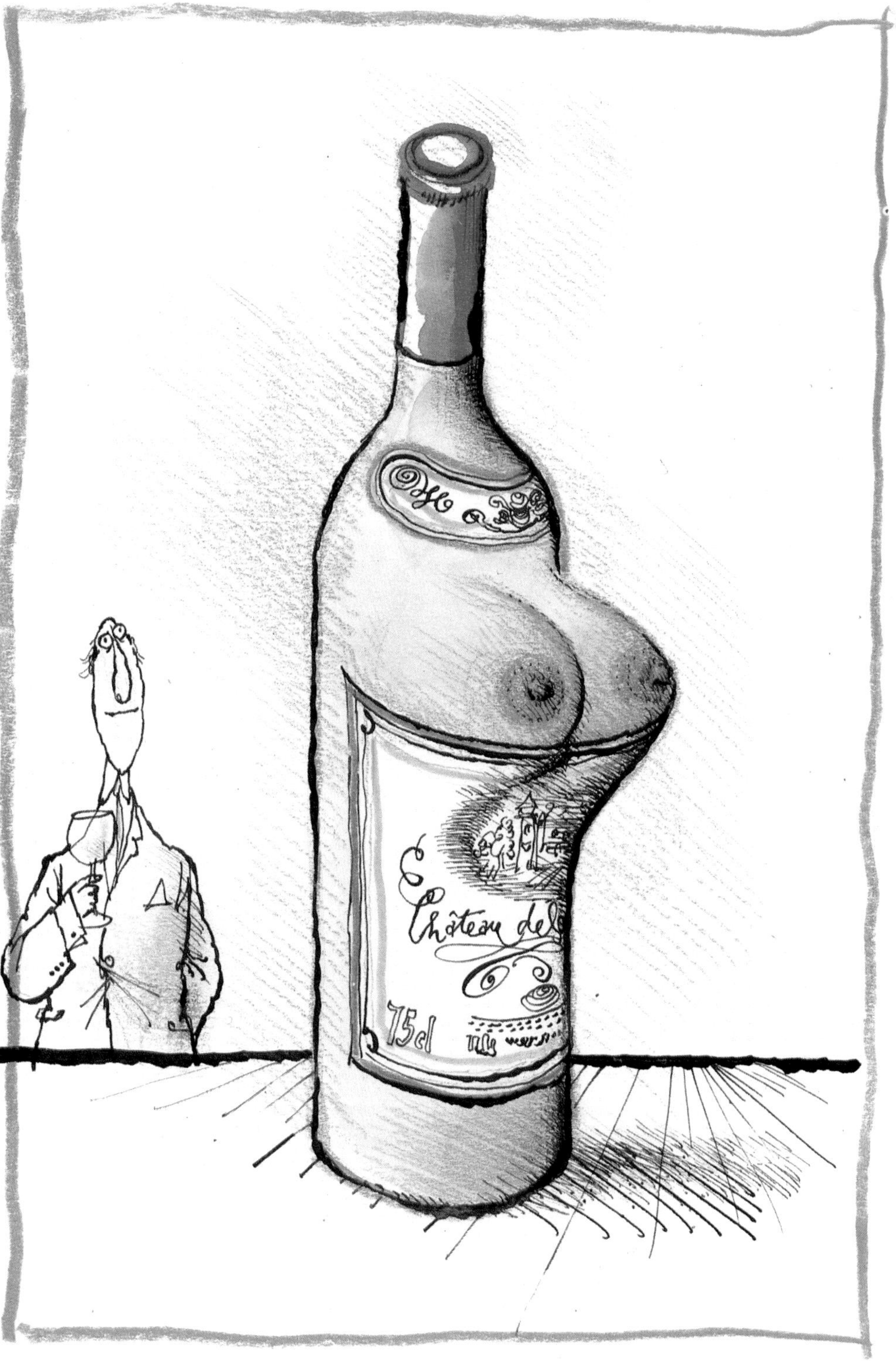
Château de
75cl

Coarse but generous

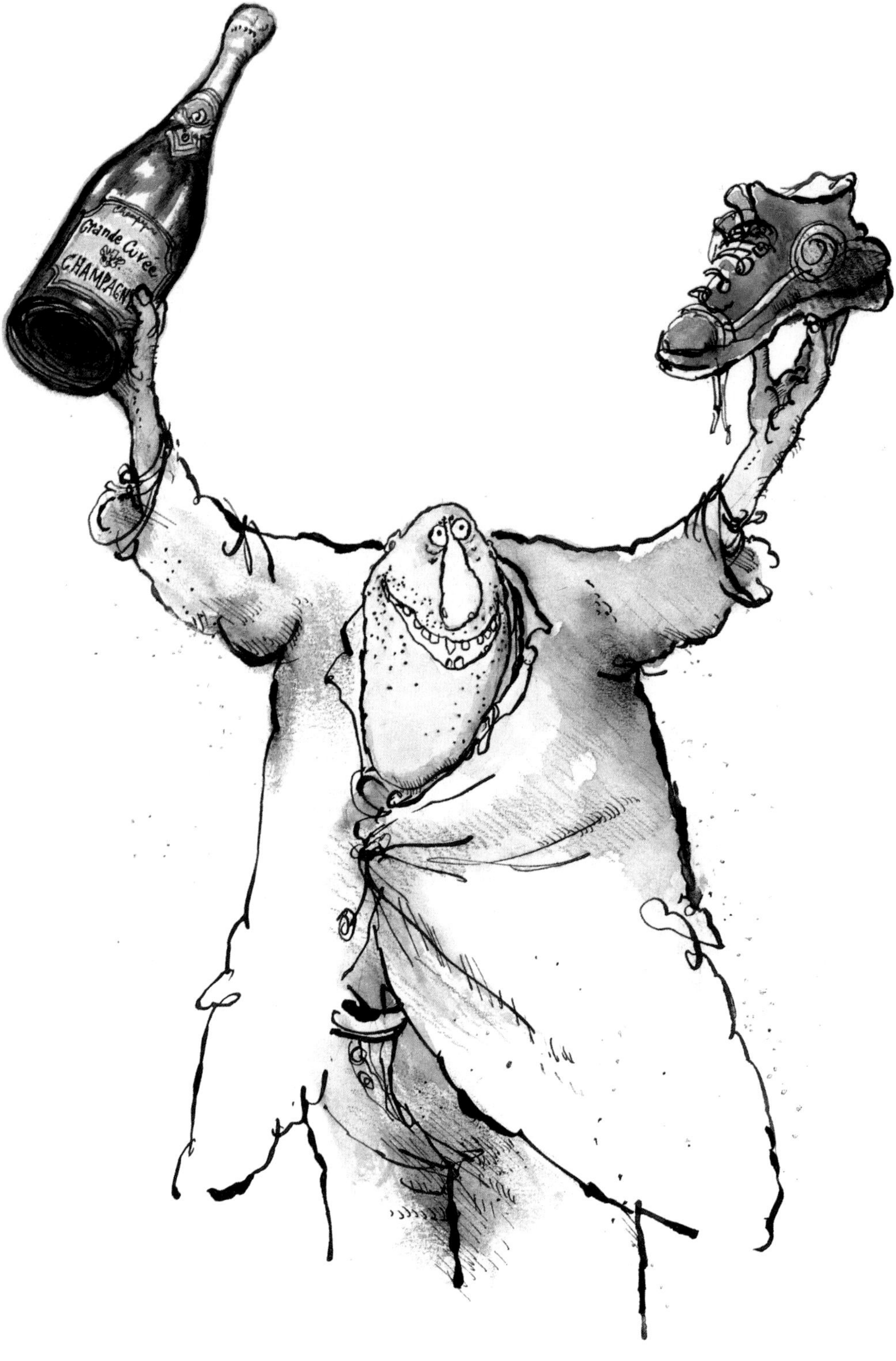
Grande Cuvée
CHAMPAGNE

Still green, but coming on nicely

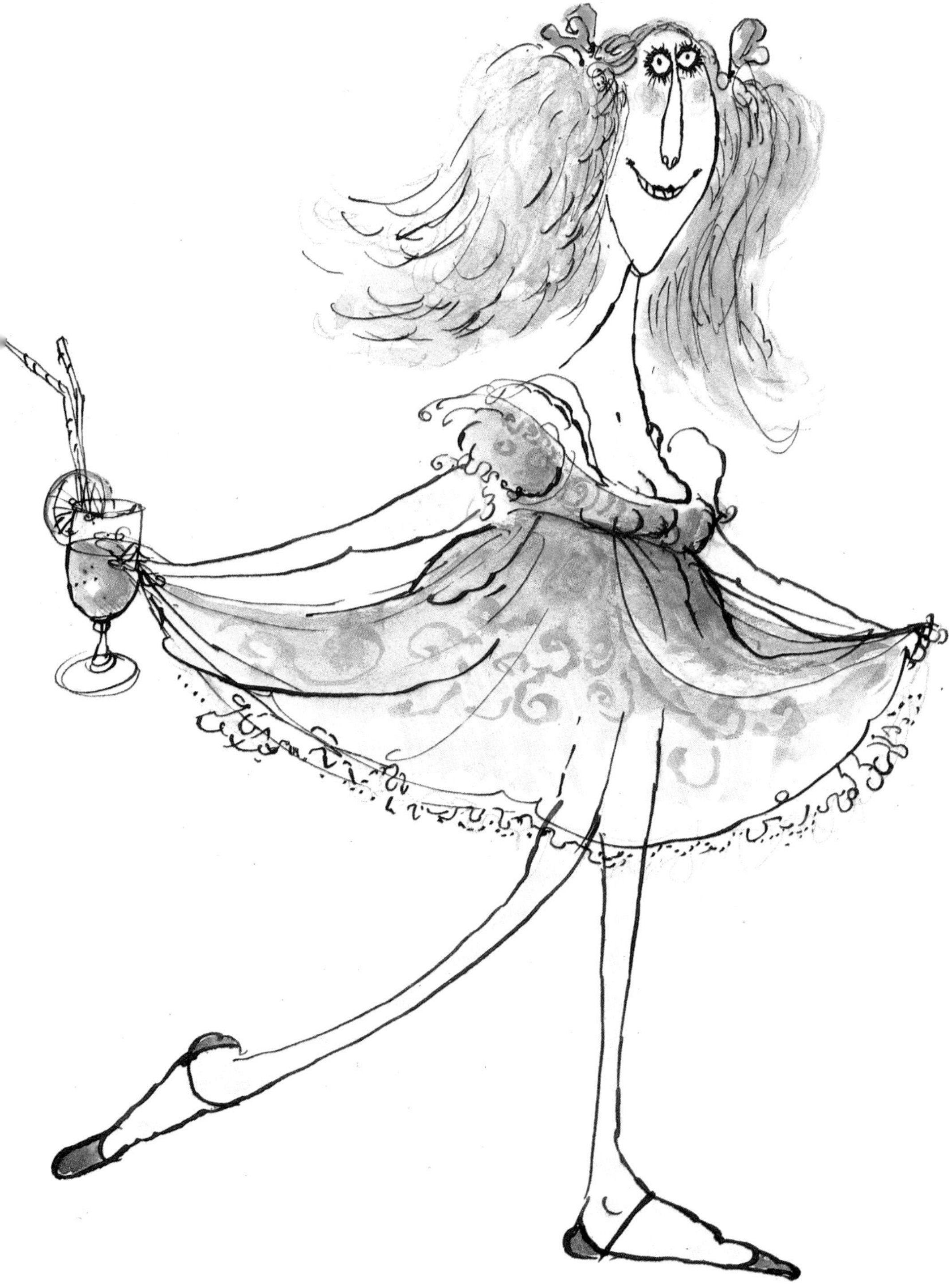

Somewhat lacking in finesse

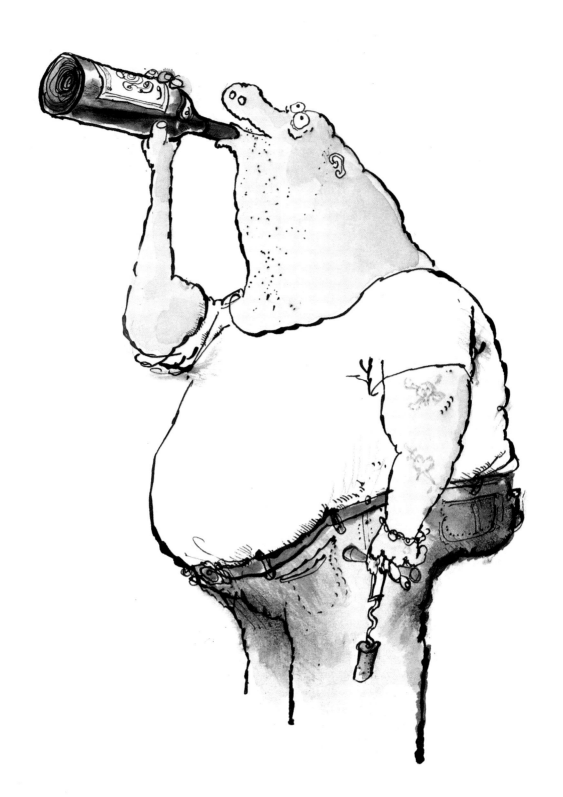

Delicately nuanced

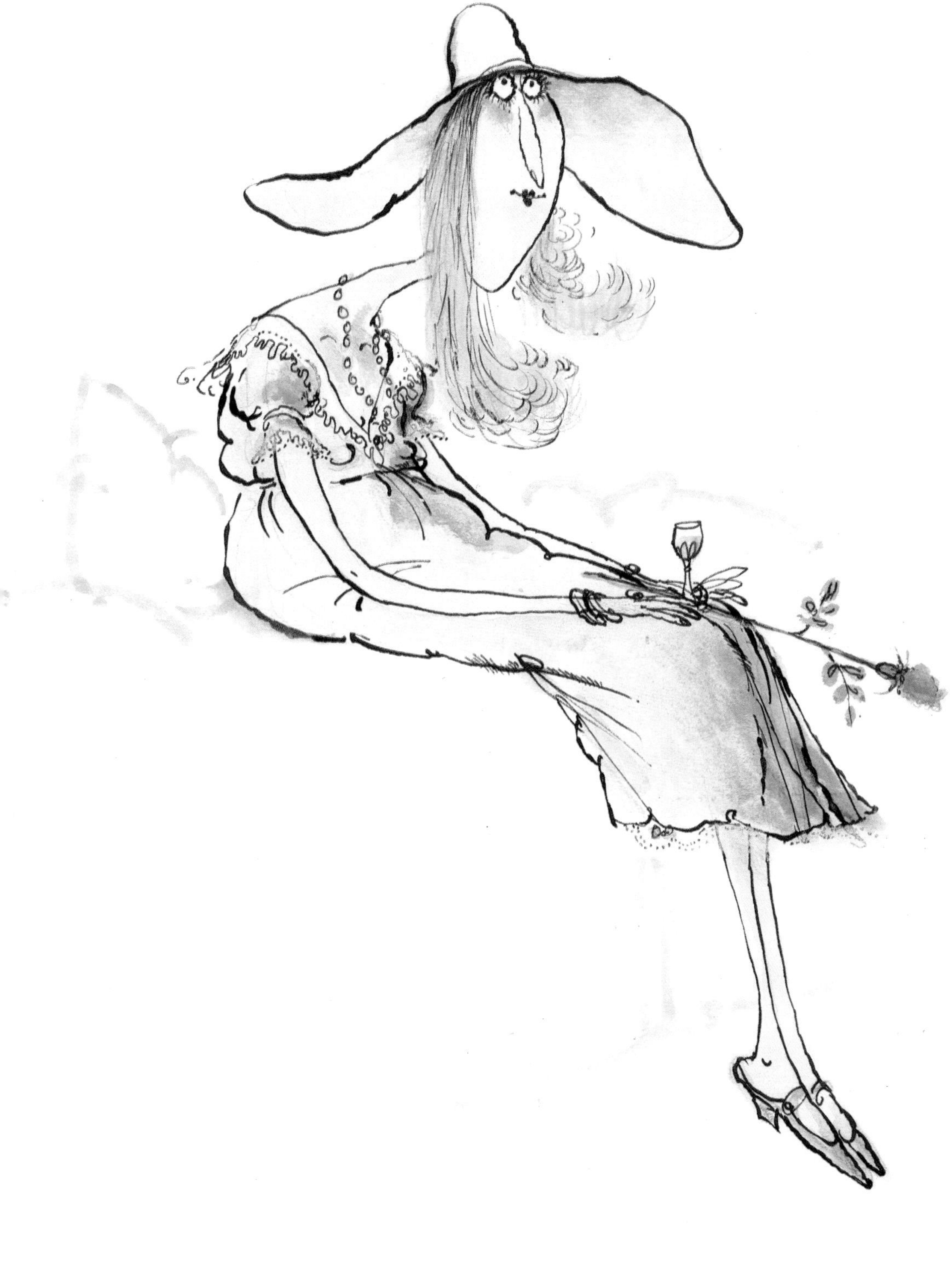

A little sullen

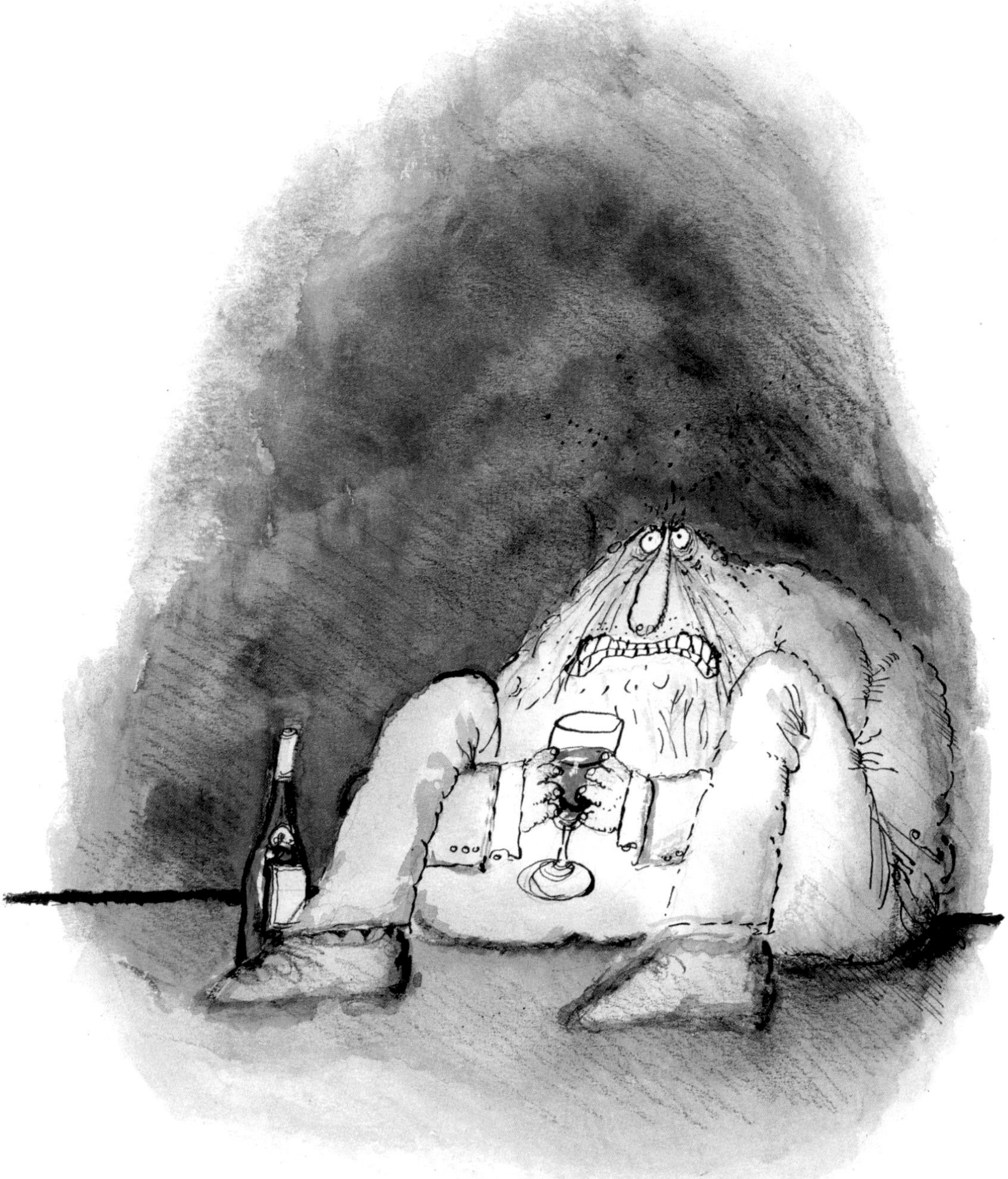

Elegant, but lacks backbone

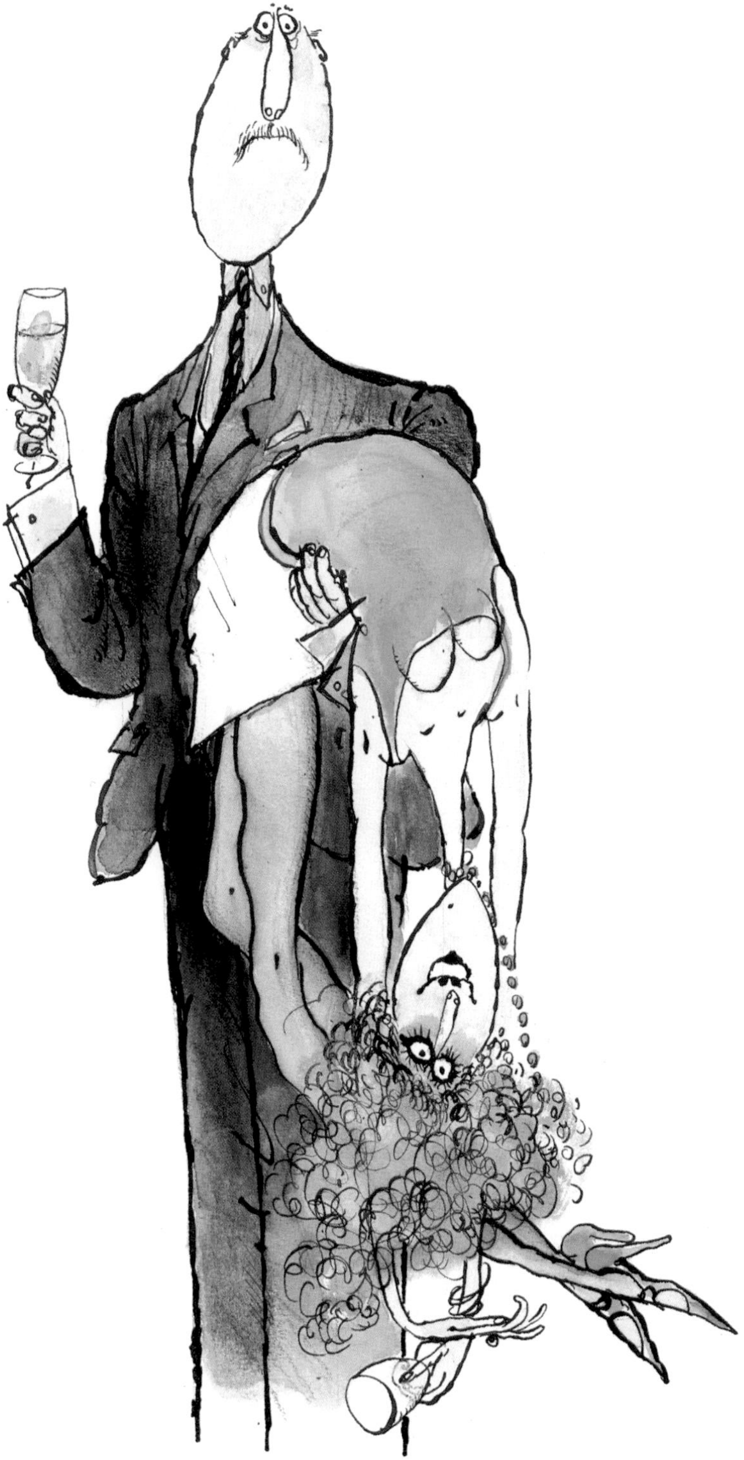

Ages beautifully

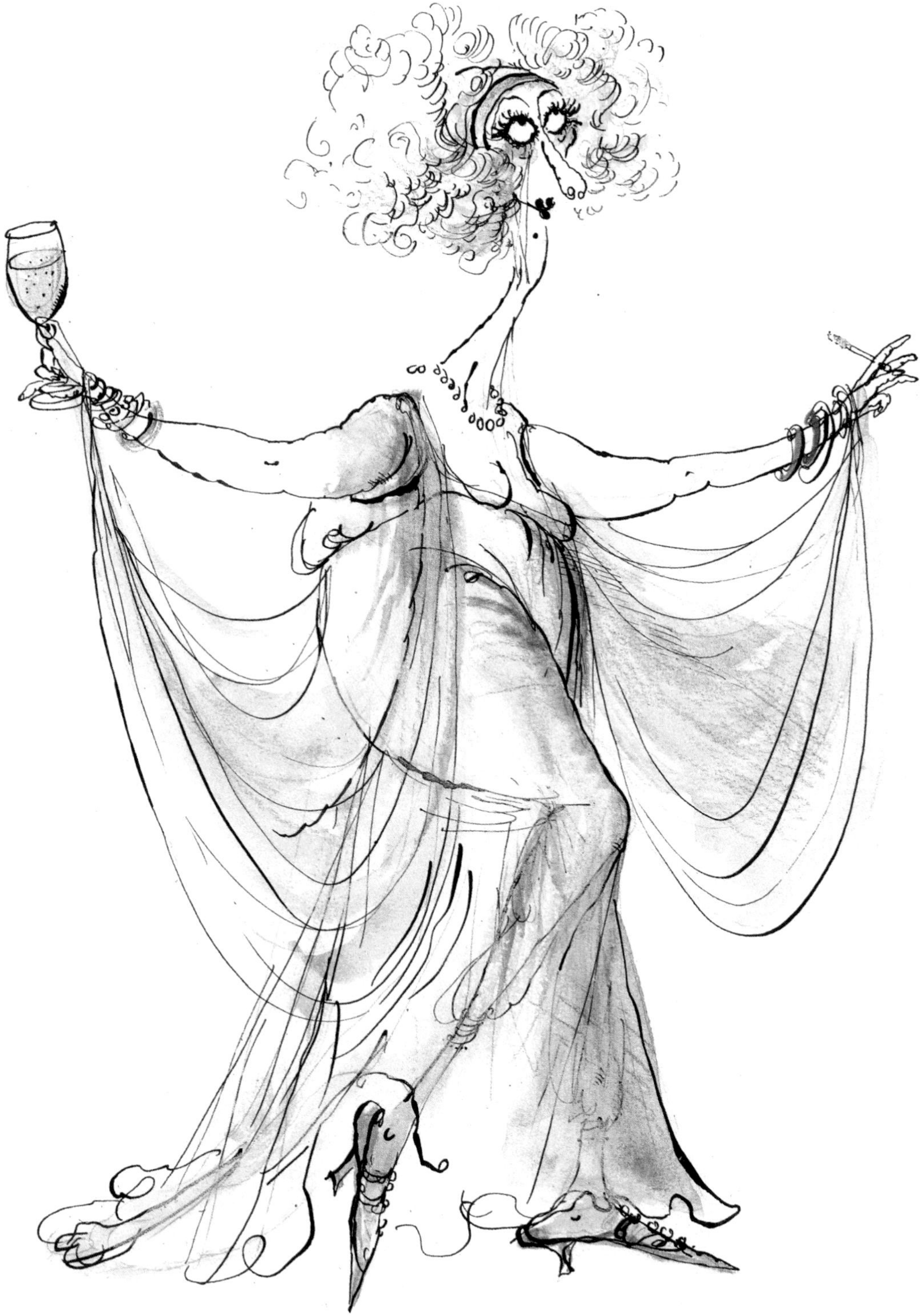

A pronounced scent of flowers

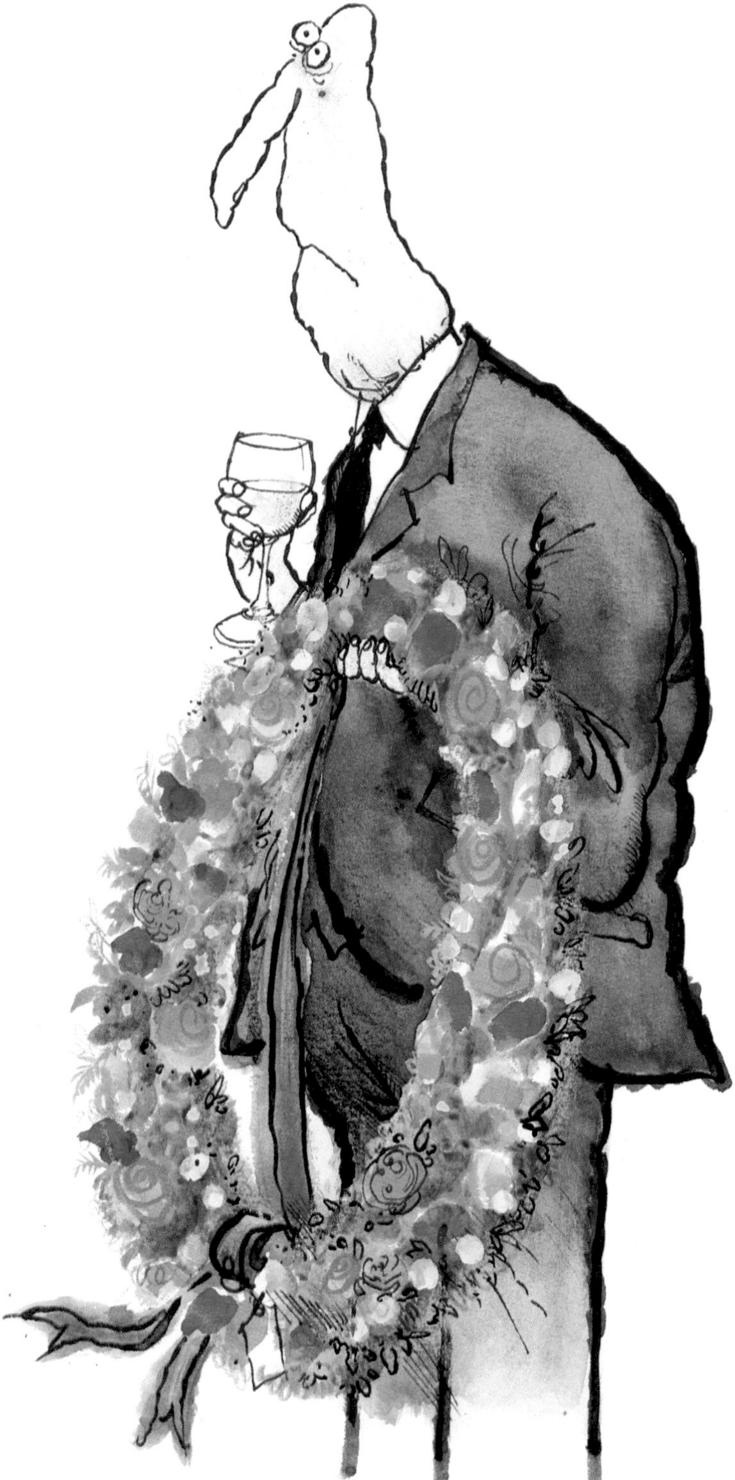

Surprisingly reticent

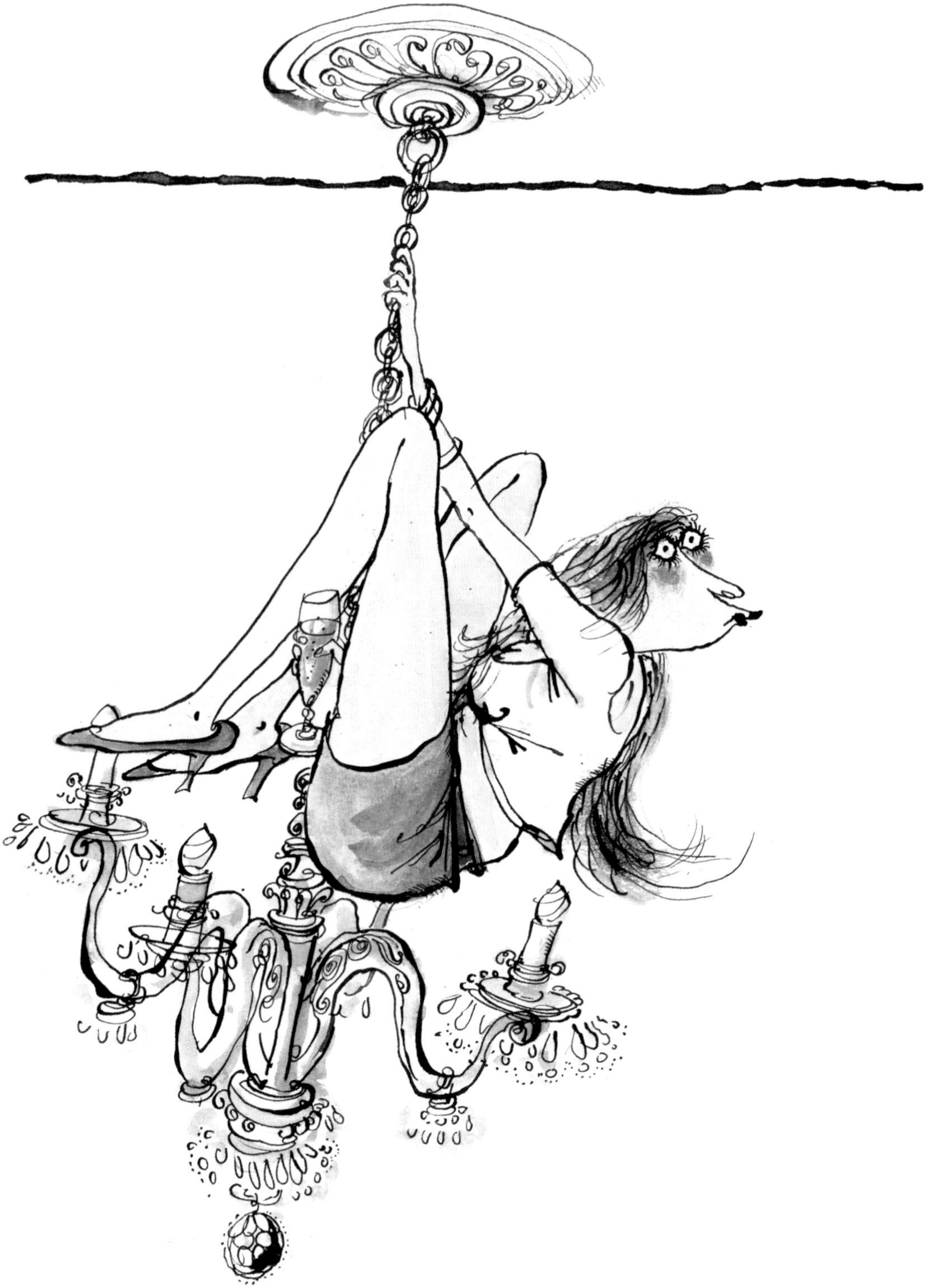

Round and supple

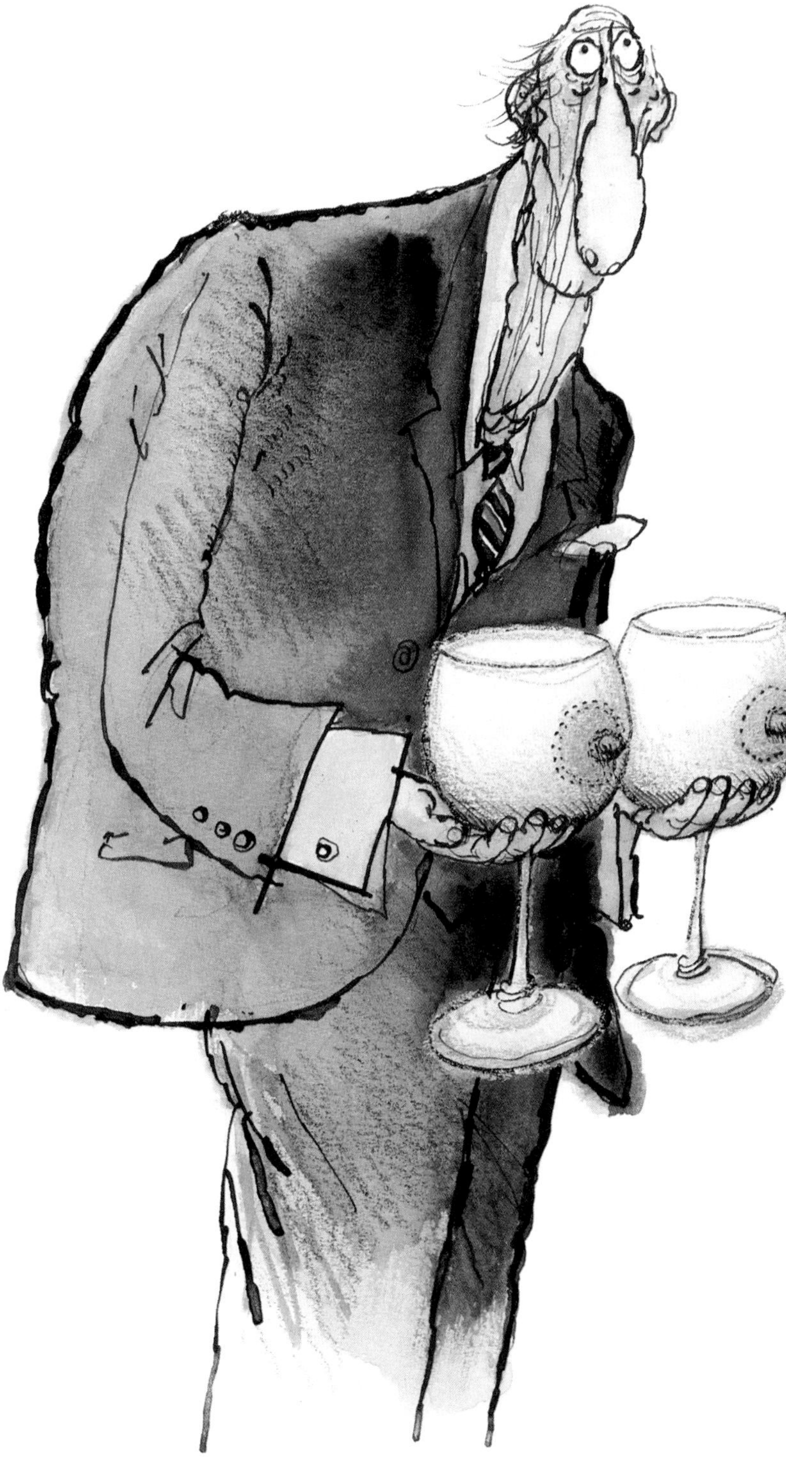

Full-bodied, with great character

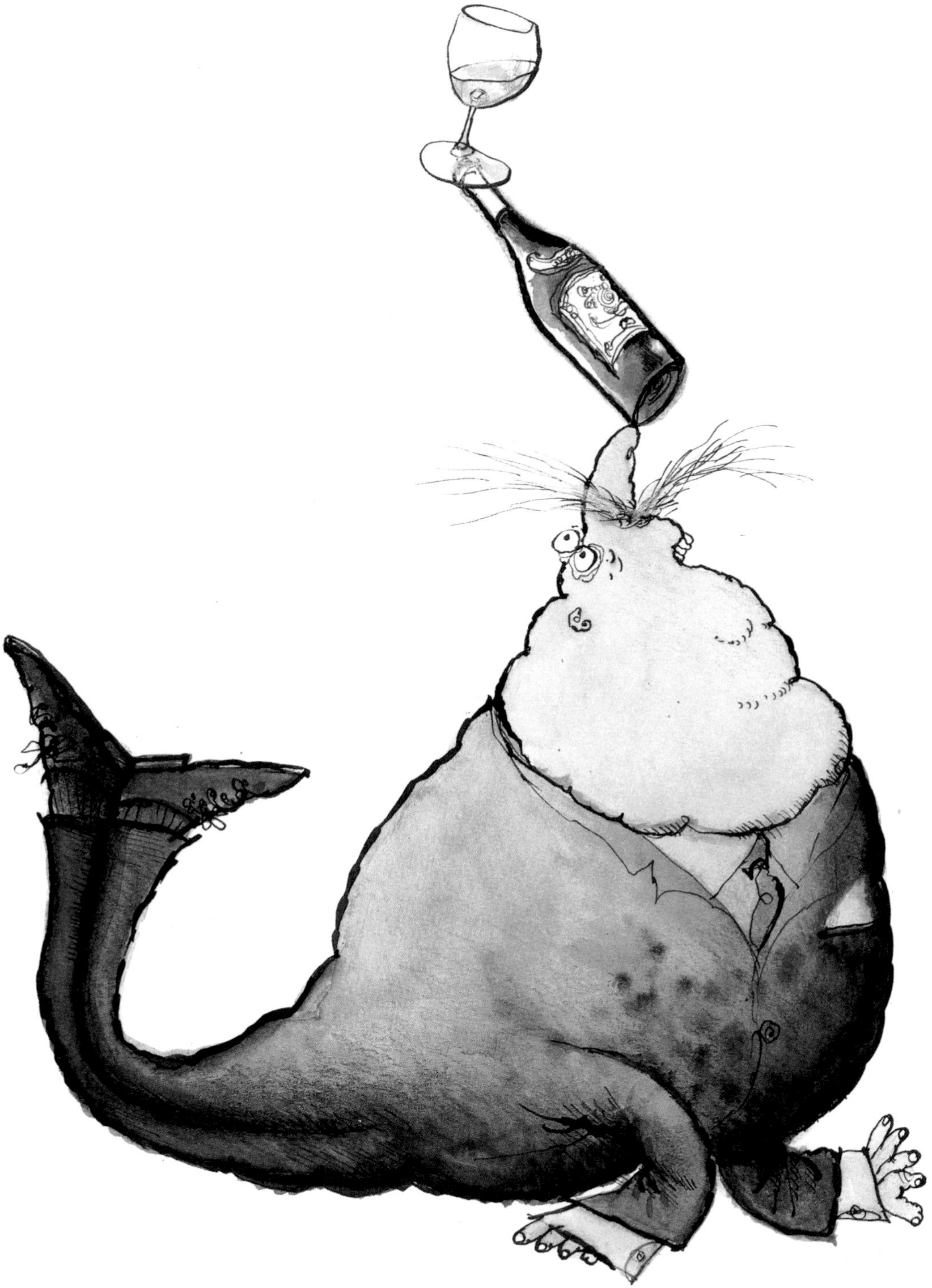

Leave to age

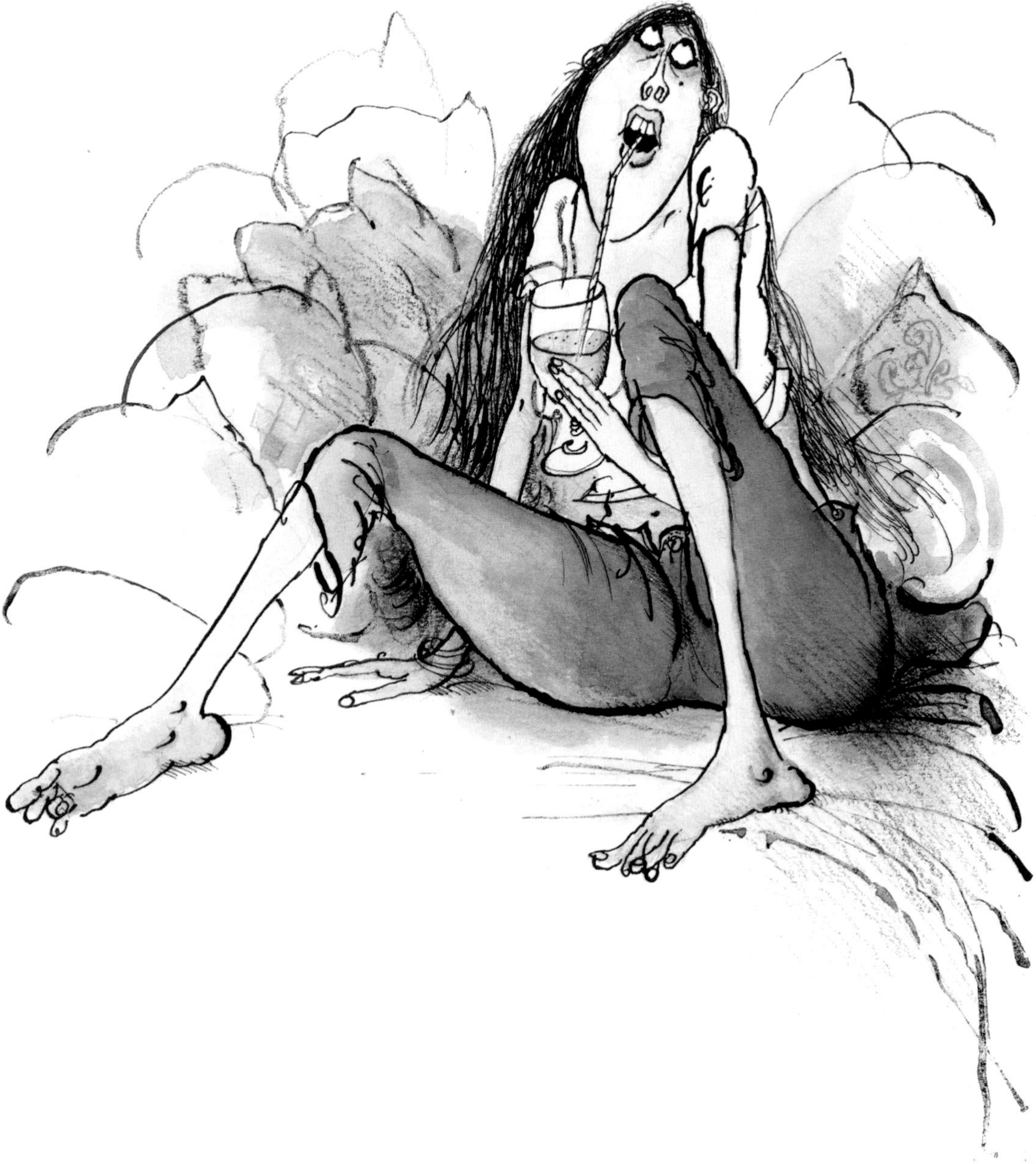

Generous and high in alcoholic content

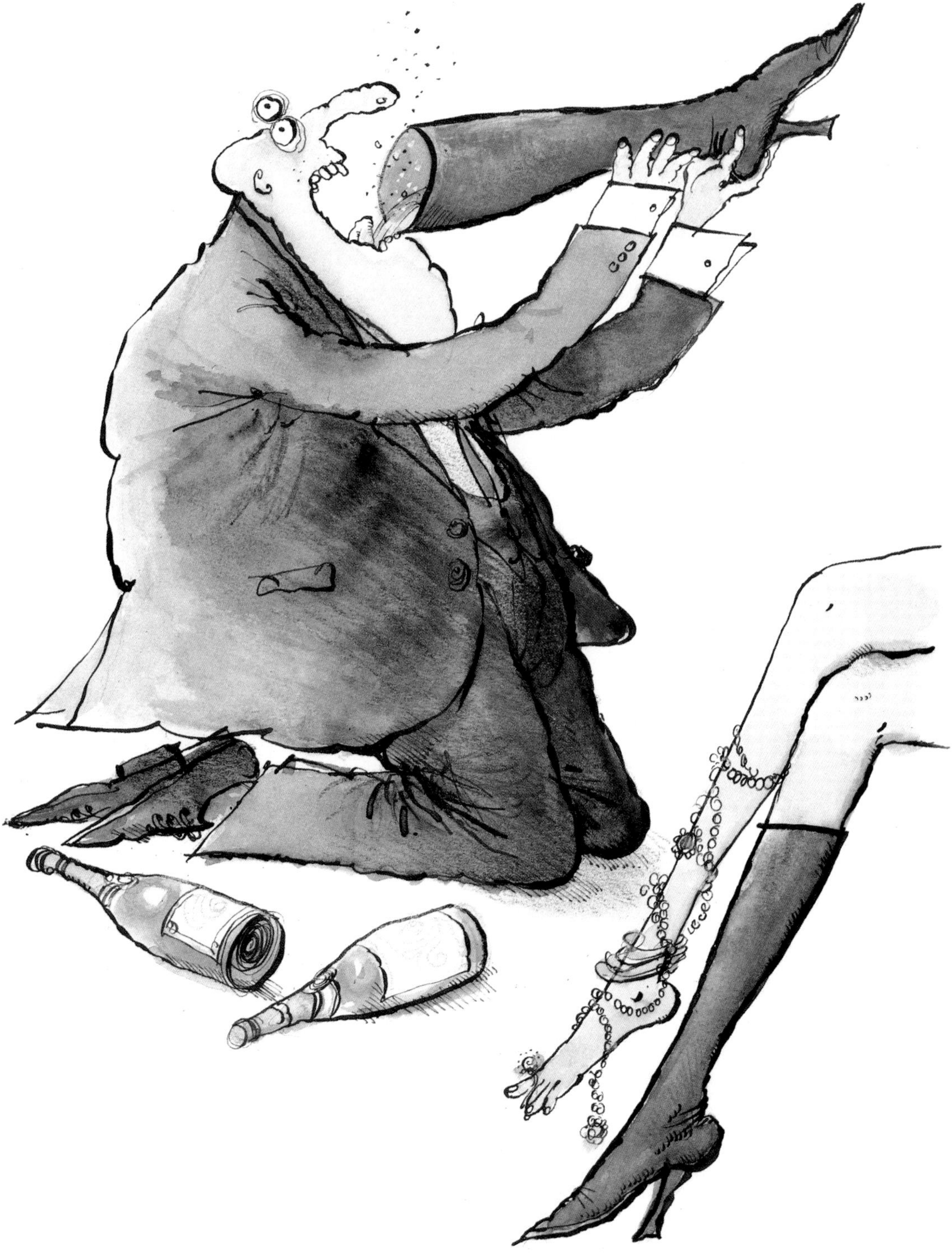

Lots of body, but supple

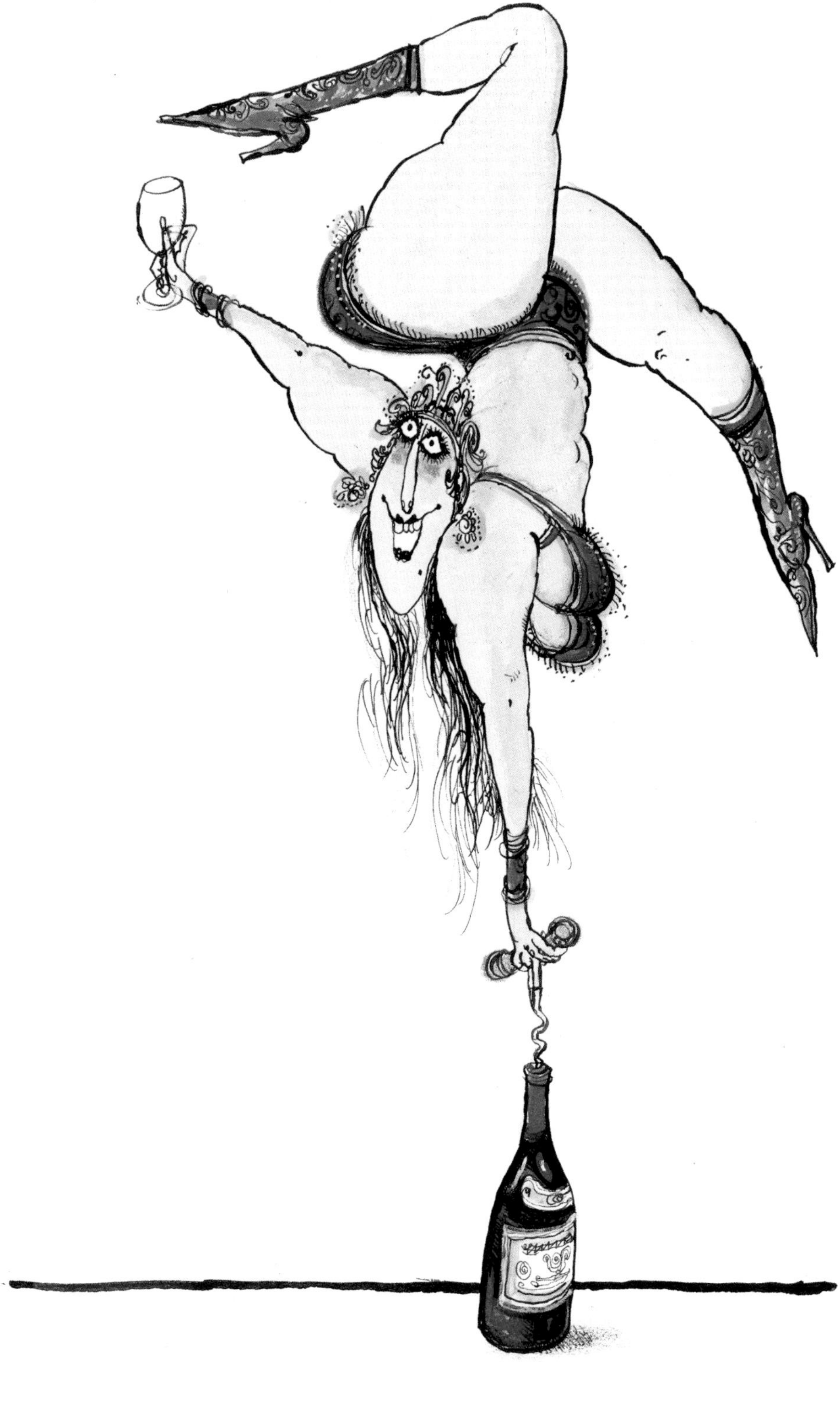

Vigorous and well constructed

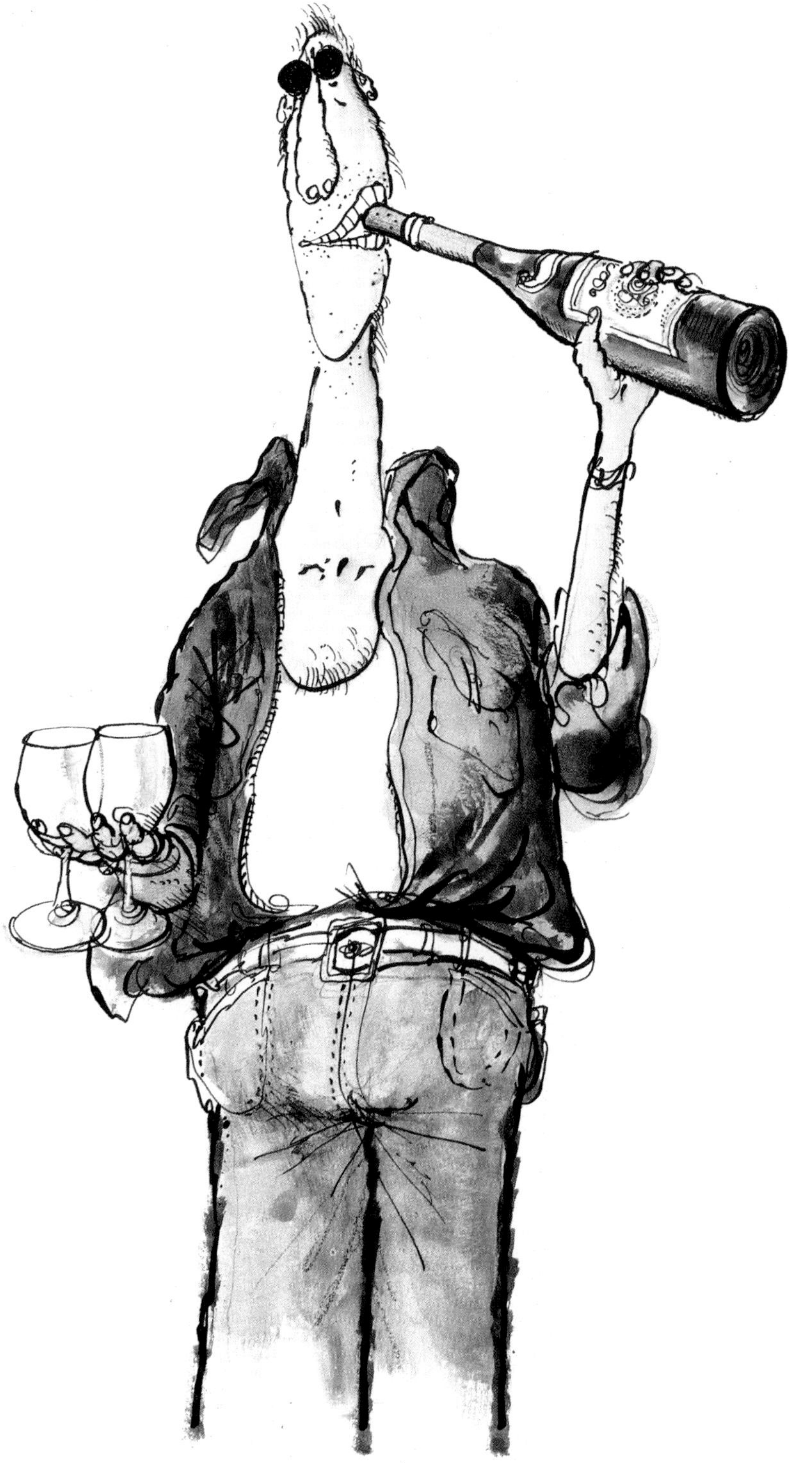

Interesting depth of flavour

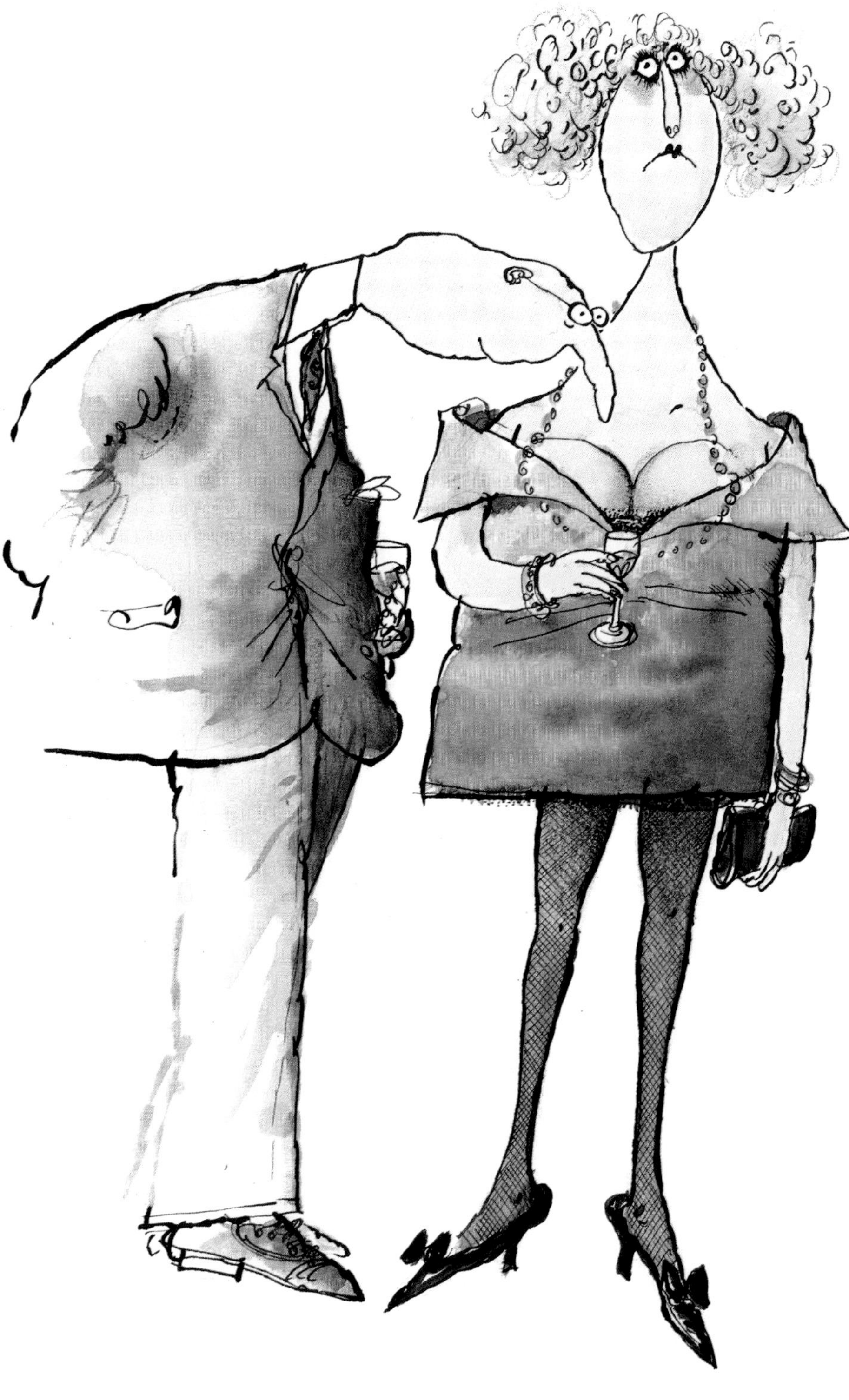

Delicate, supple and flowing

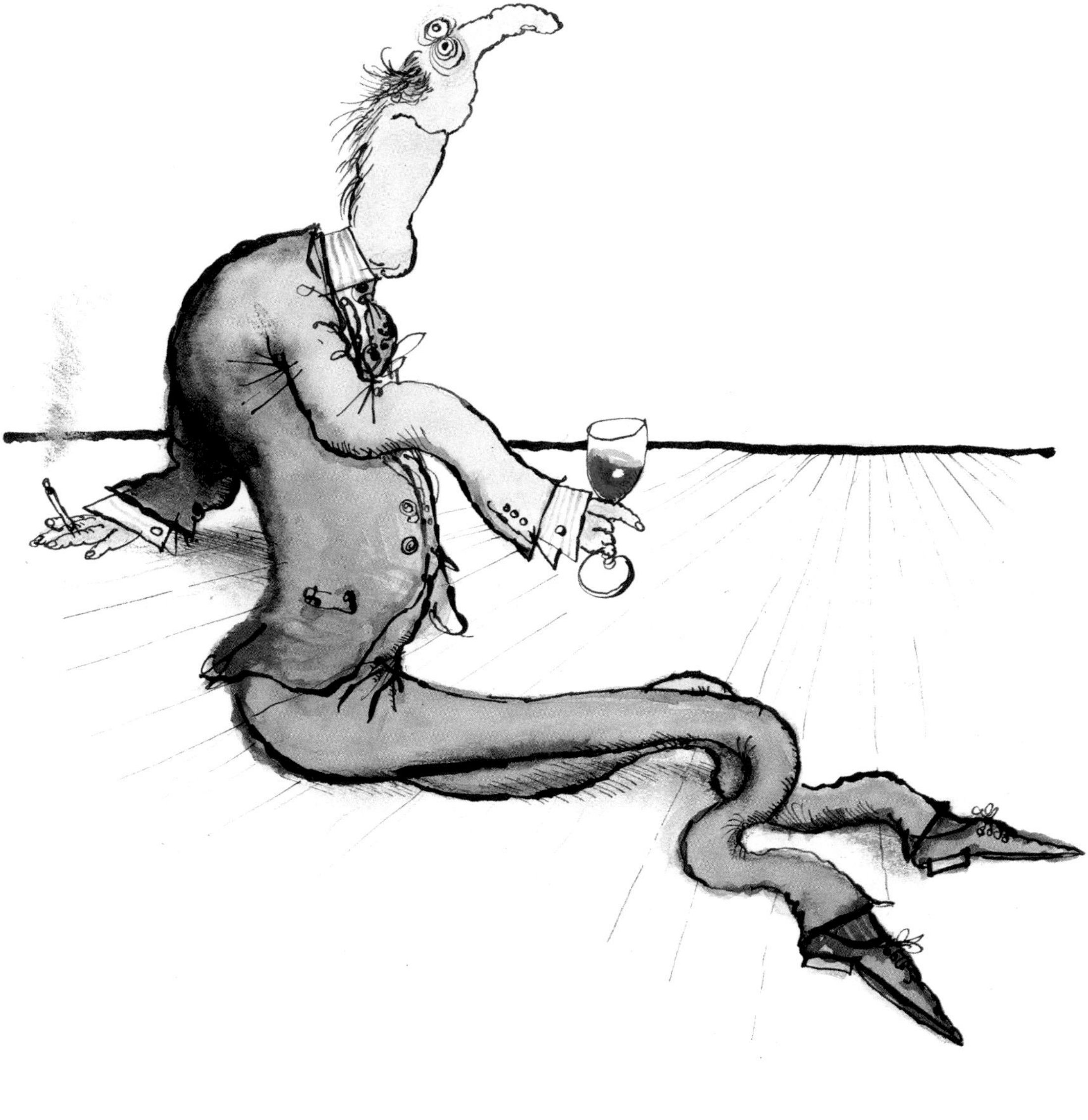

Overripeness coupled with some tartness

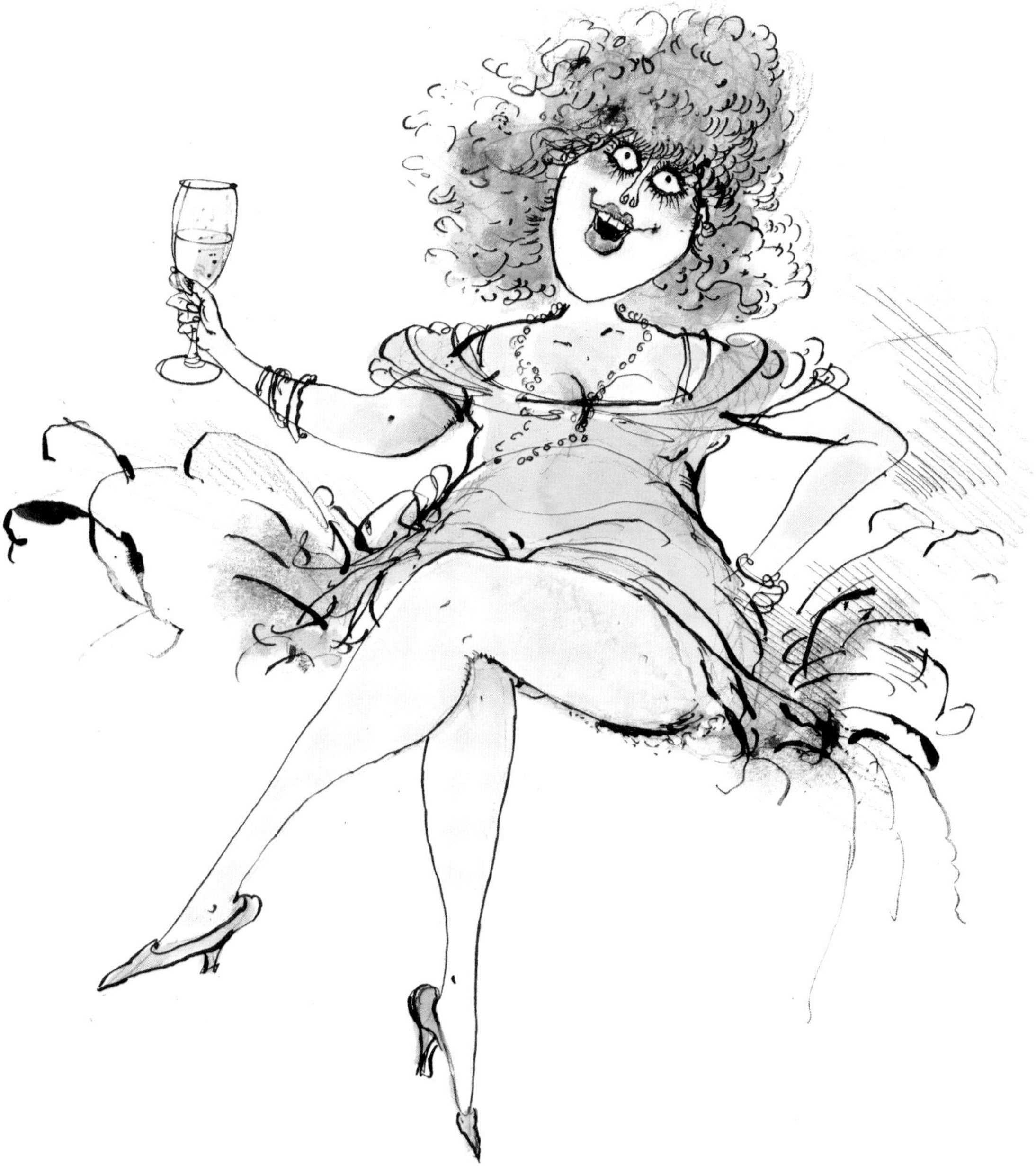

Lacks subtlety

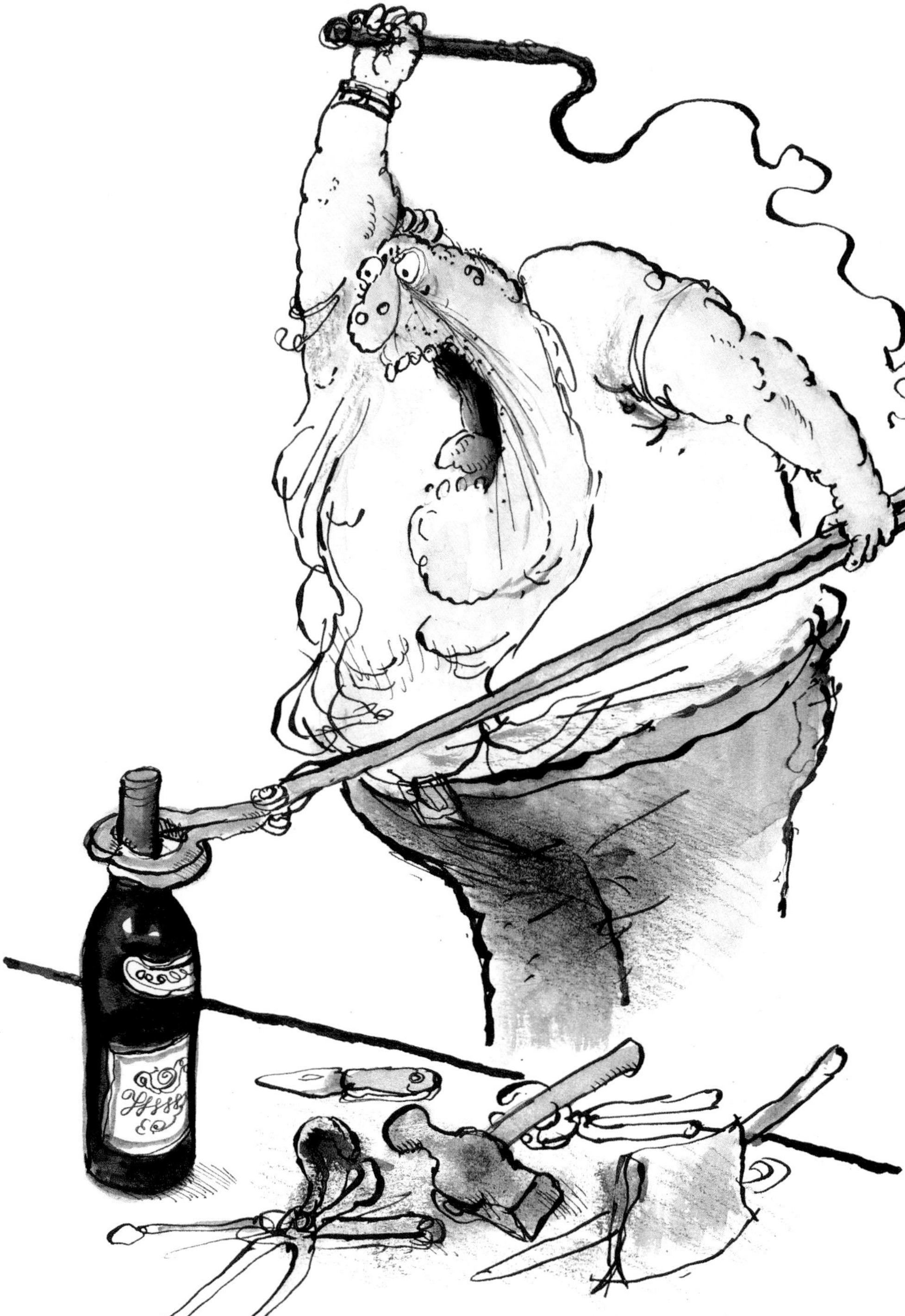

On the light and forward side

.

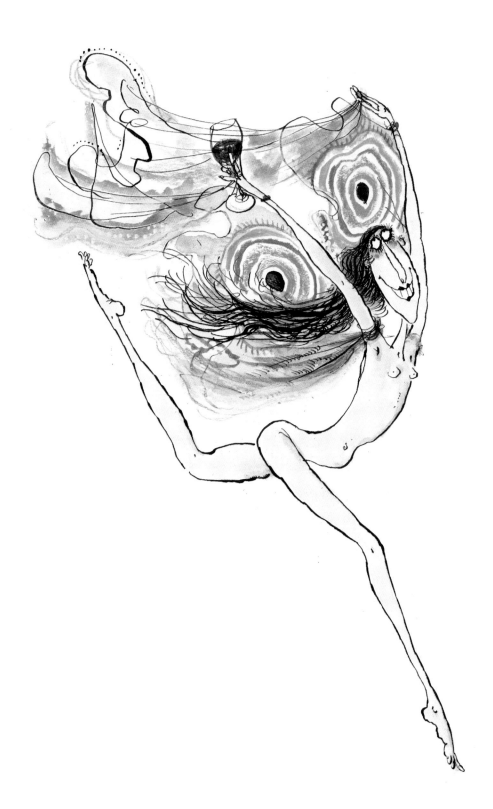

Faint touch of bitterness

Haunting aroma

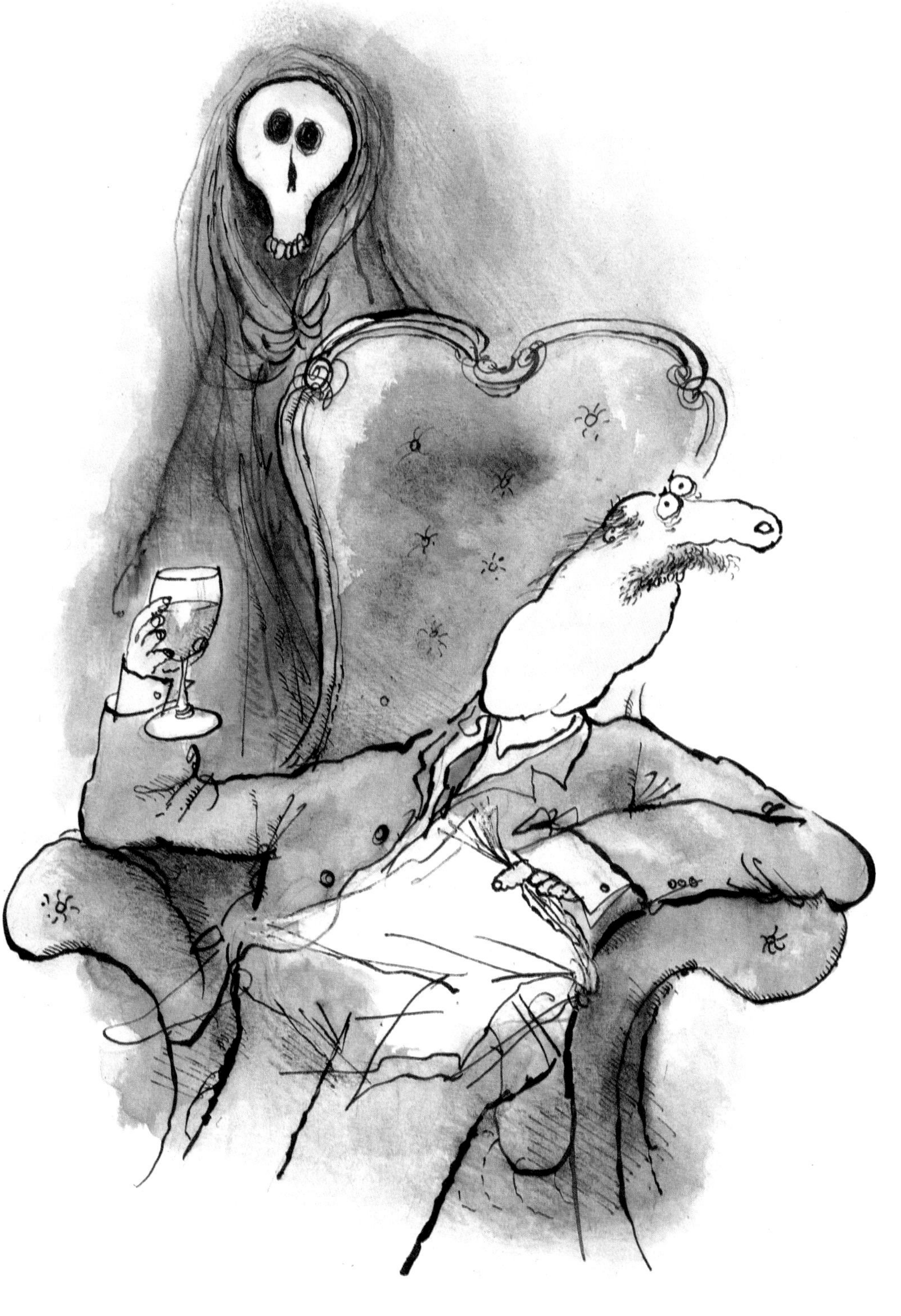

Dry, nervous, vigorous

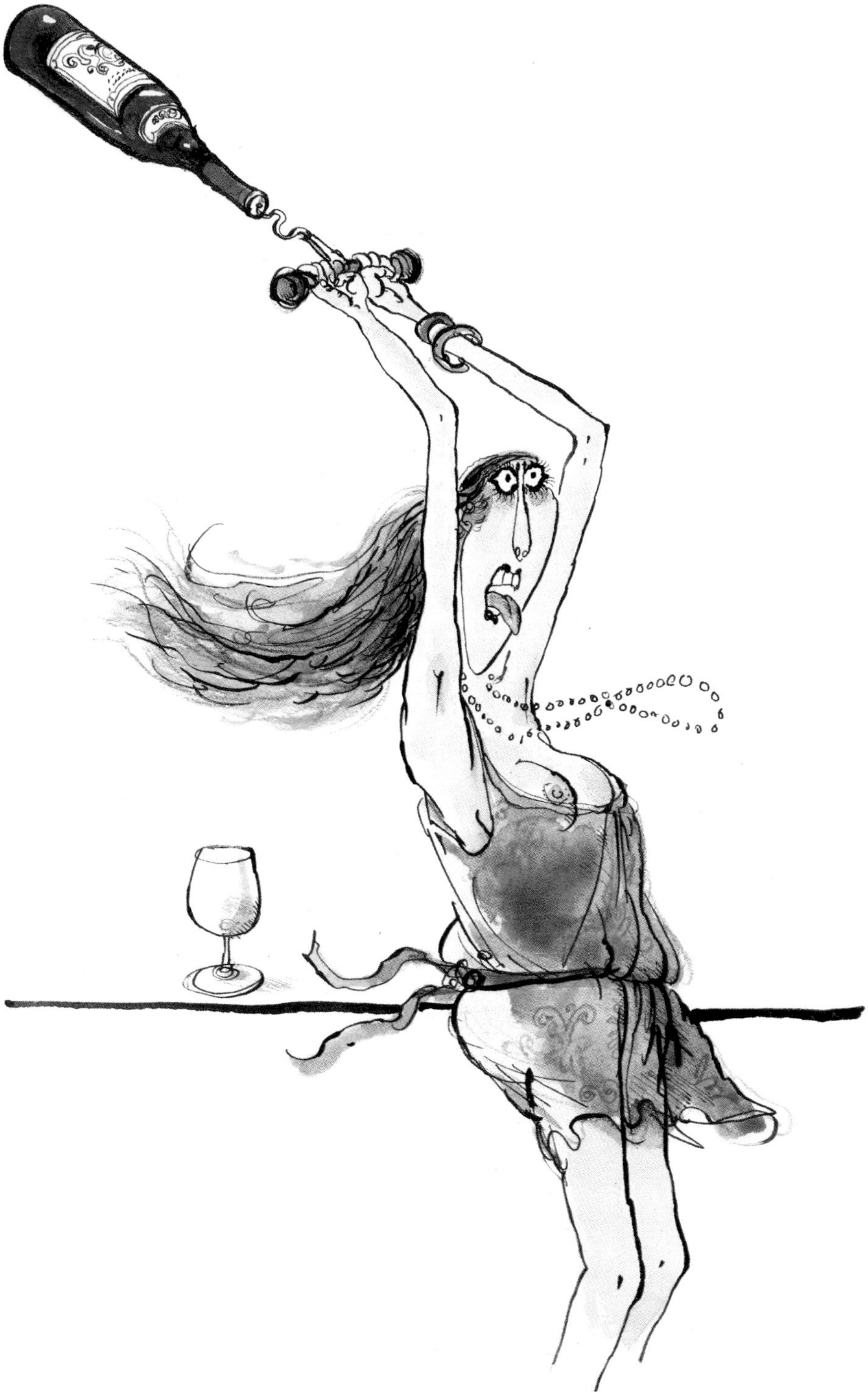

A discernible touch of oak

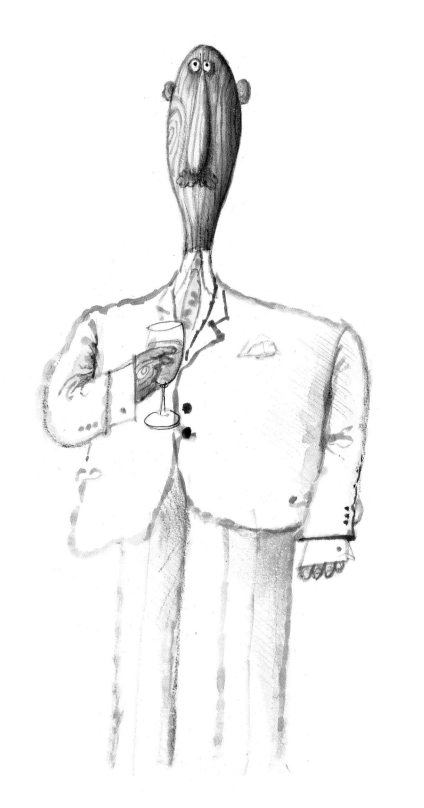

Delightfully smoky aftertaste

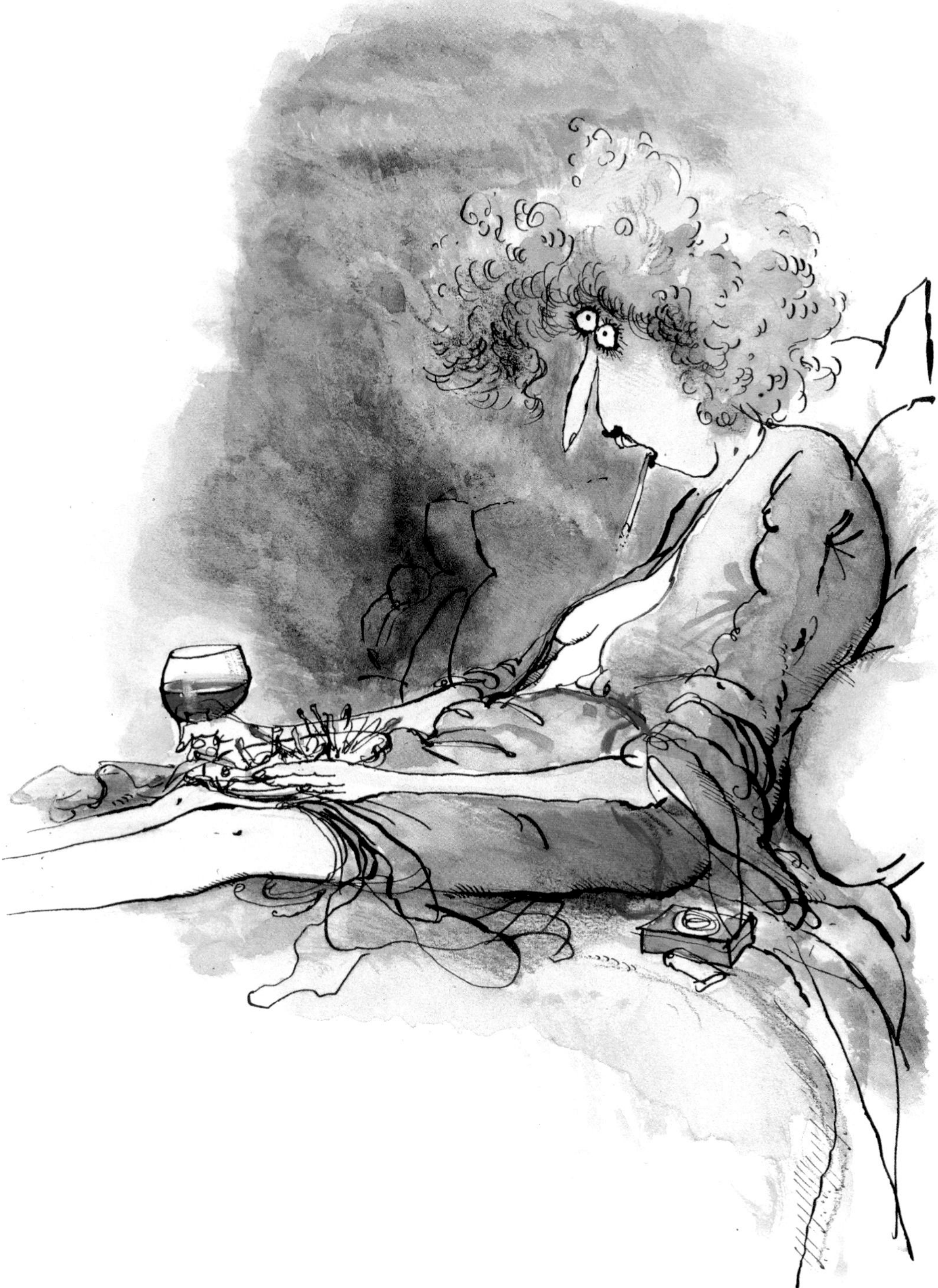

Lots of class and much in demand

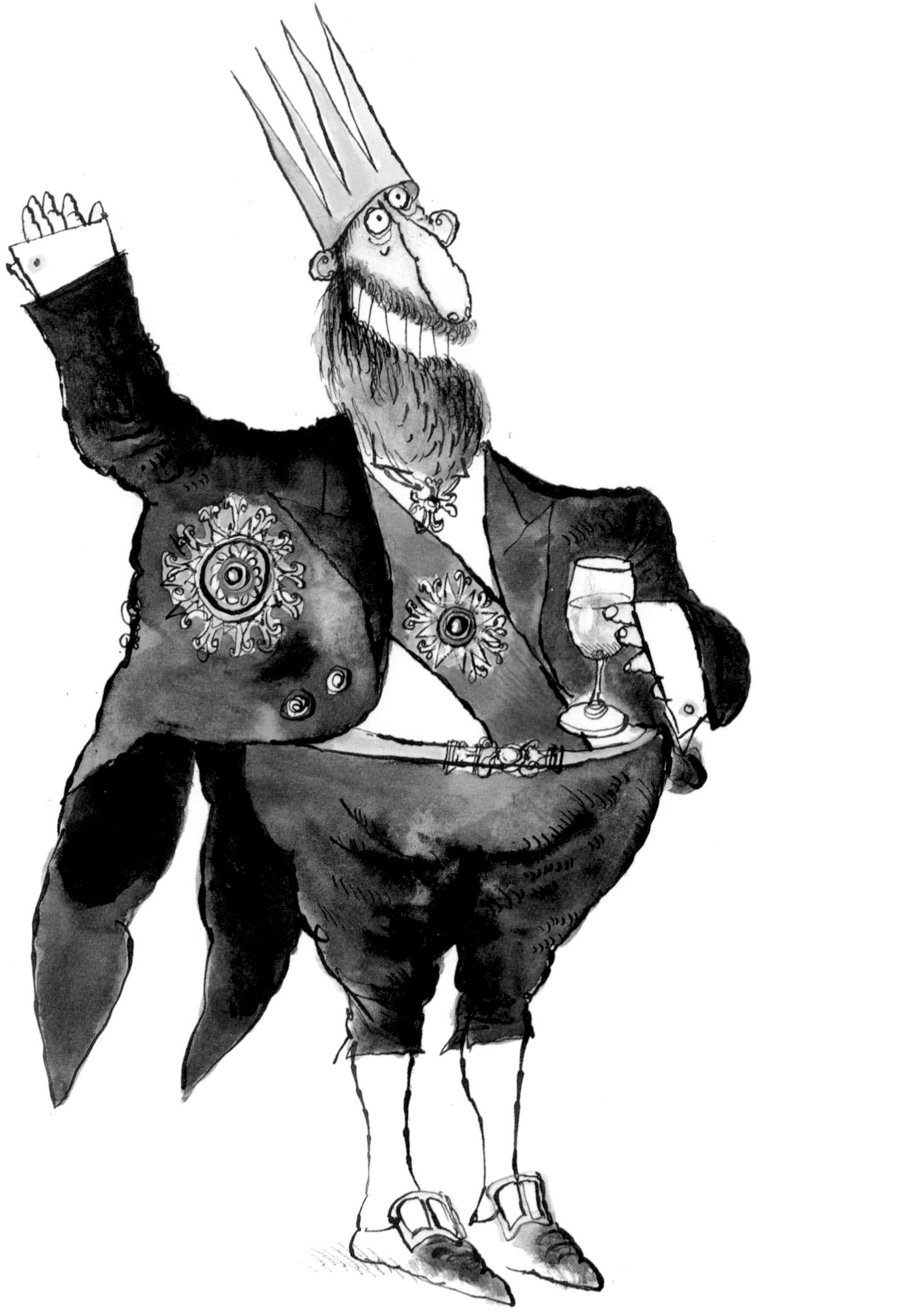

Really quite forward

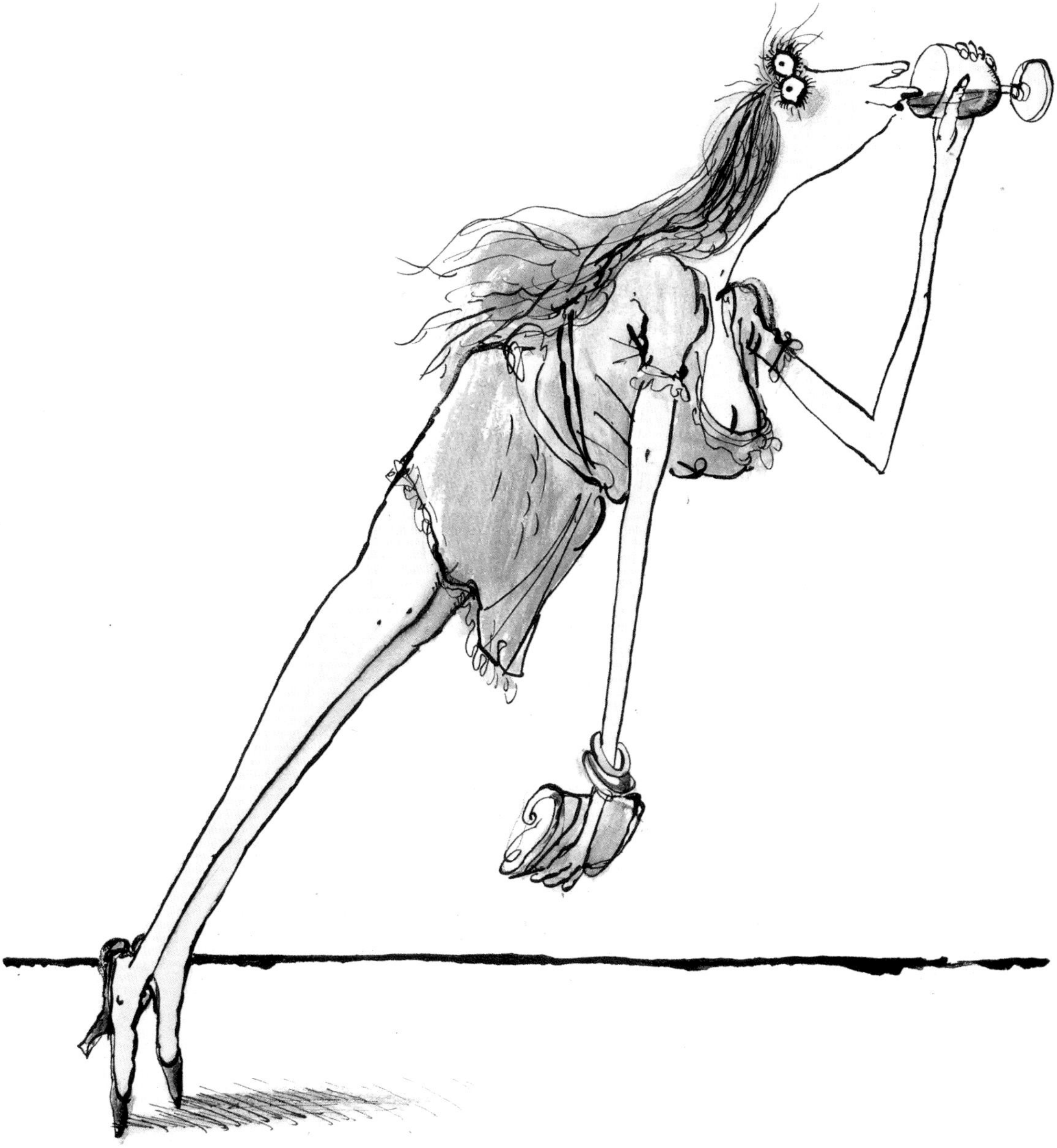

Full, fruity character

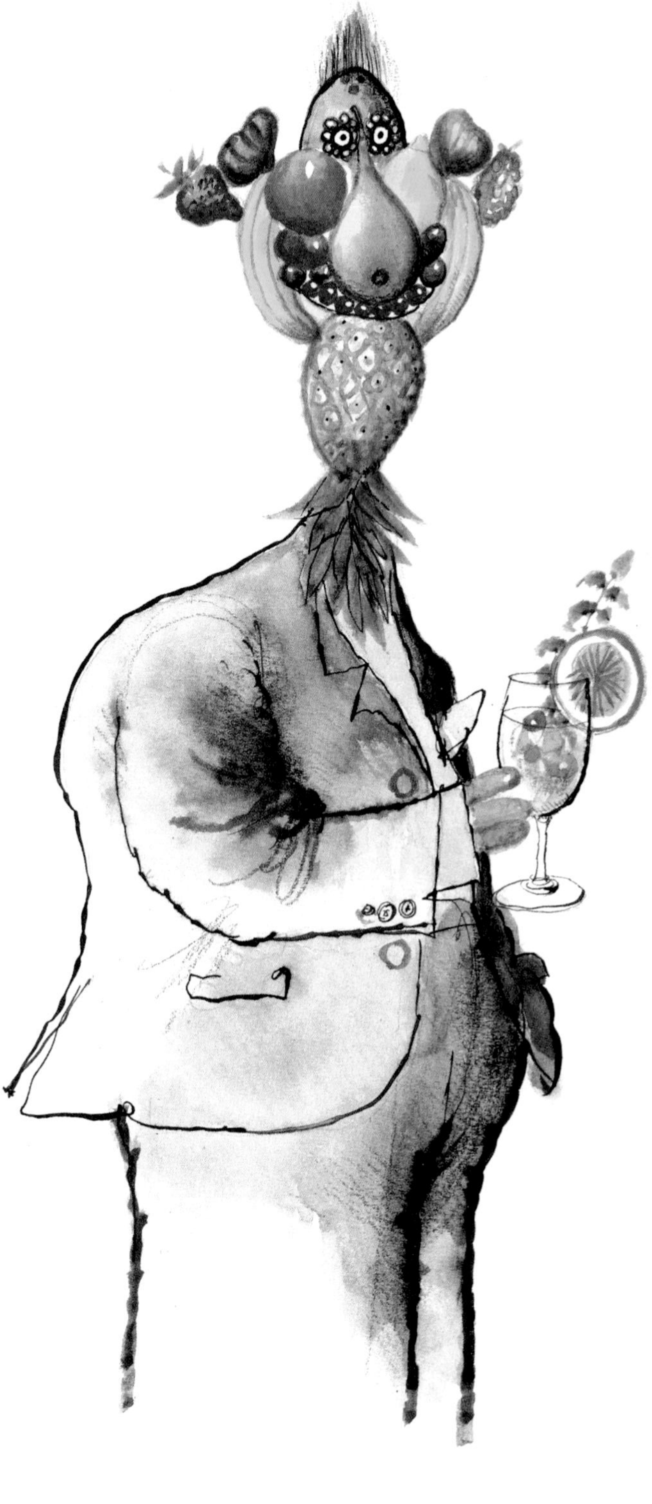

Ripe, but lacks concentration

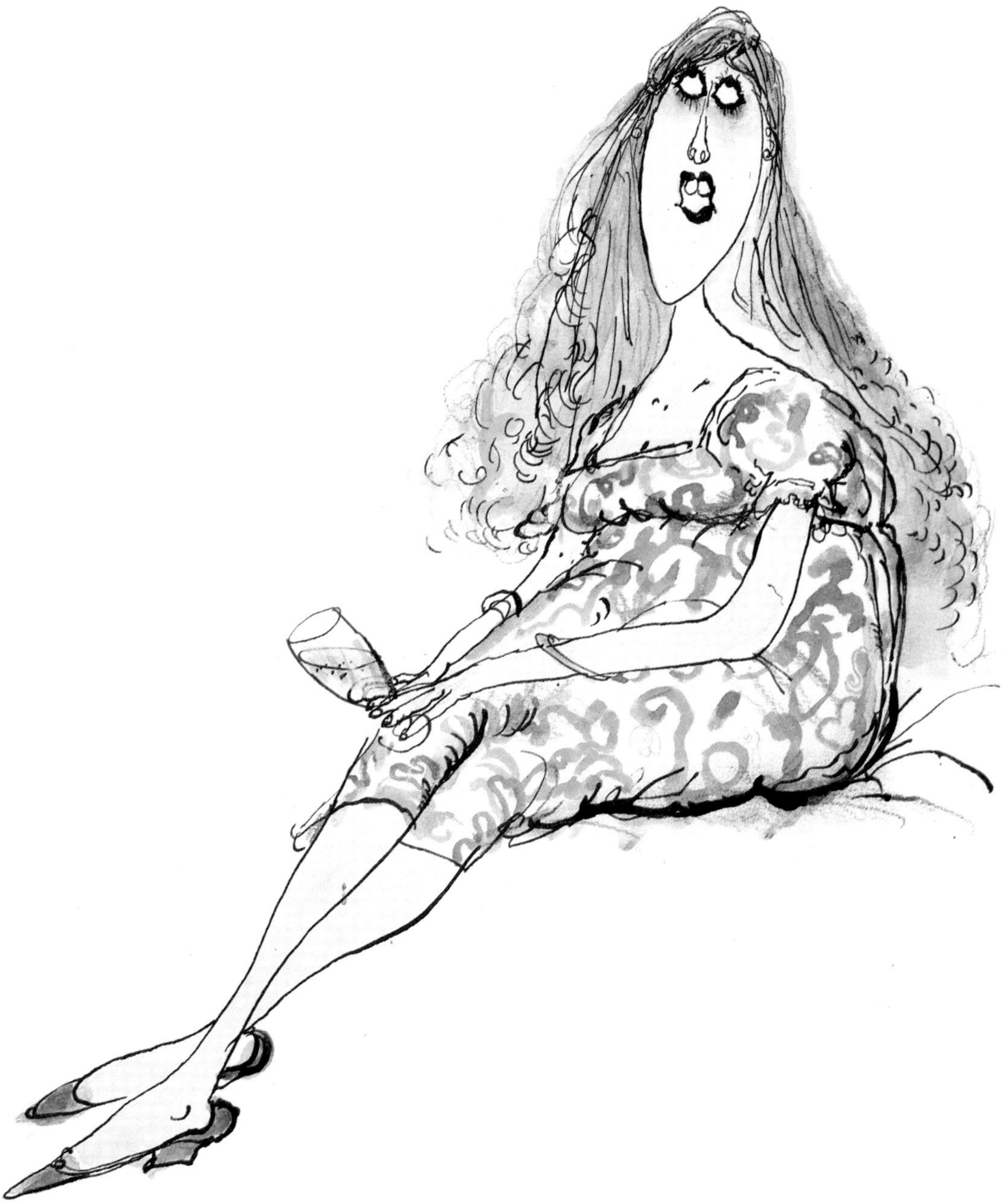

Will gain much charm with time

Has undergone noble rot

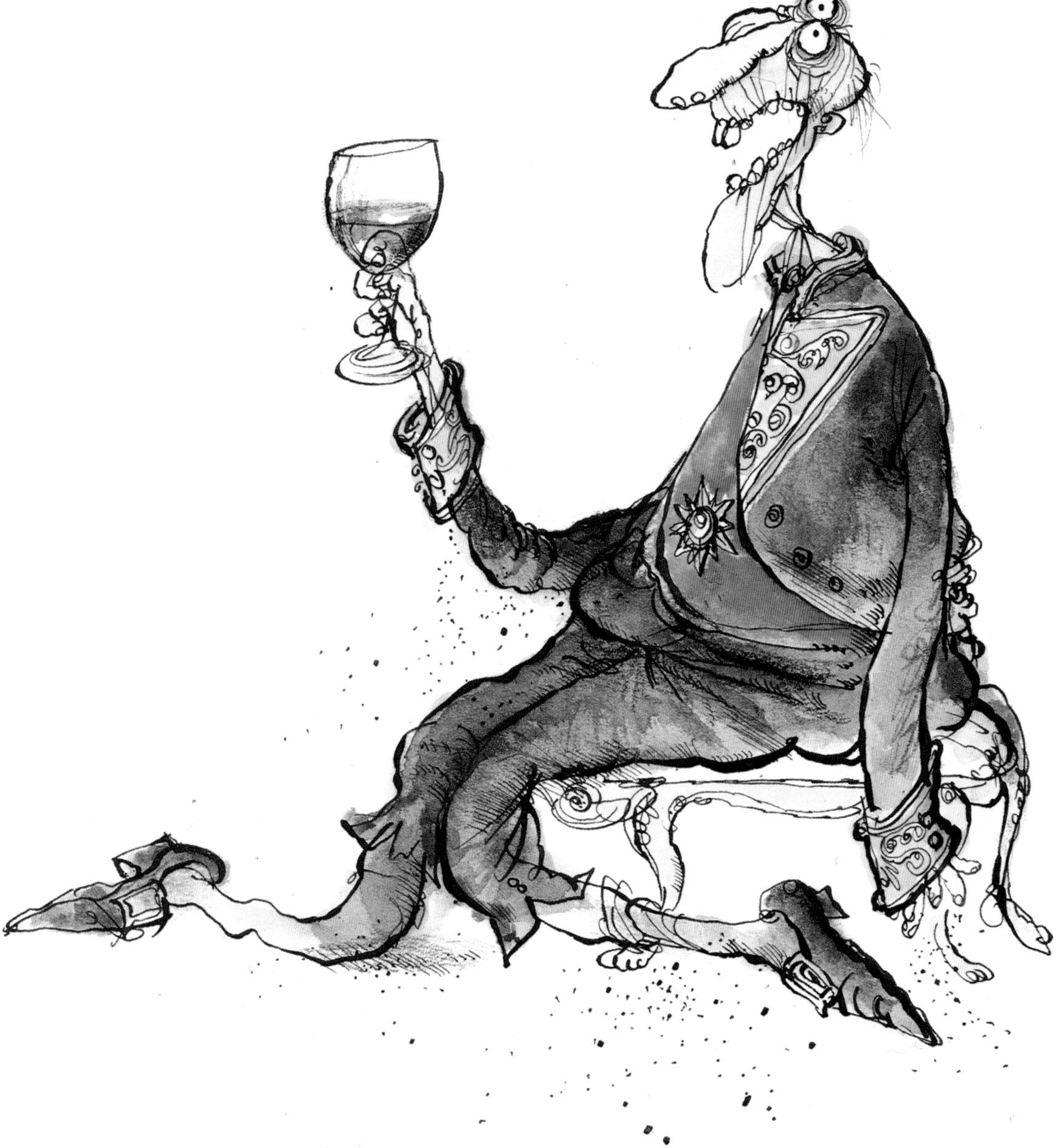

Healthy, but a bit sweaty

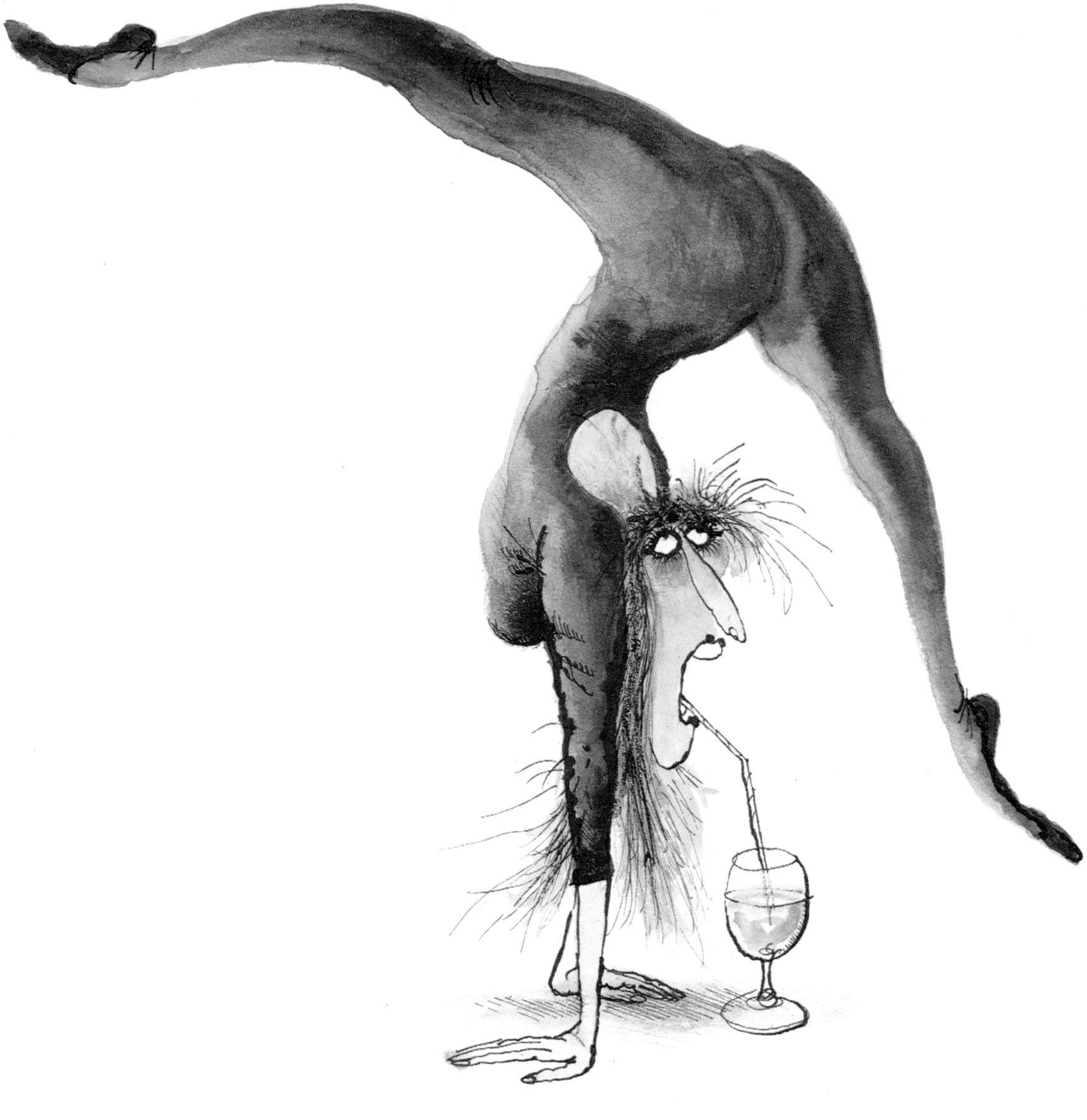

The nose is fantastic

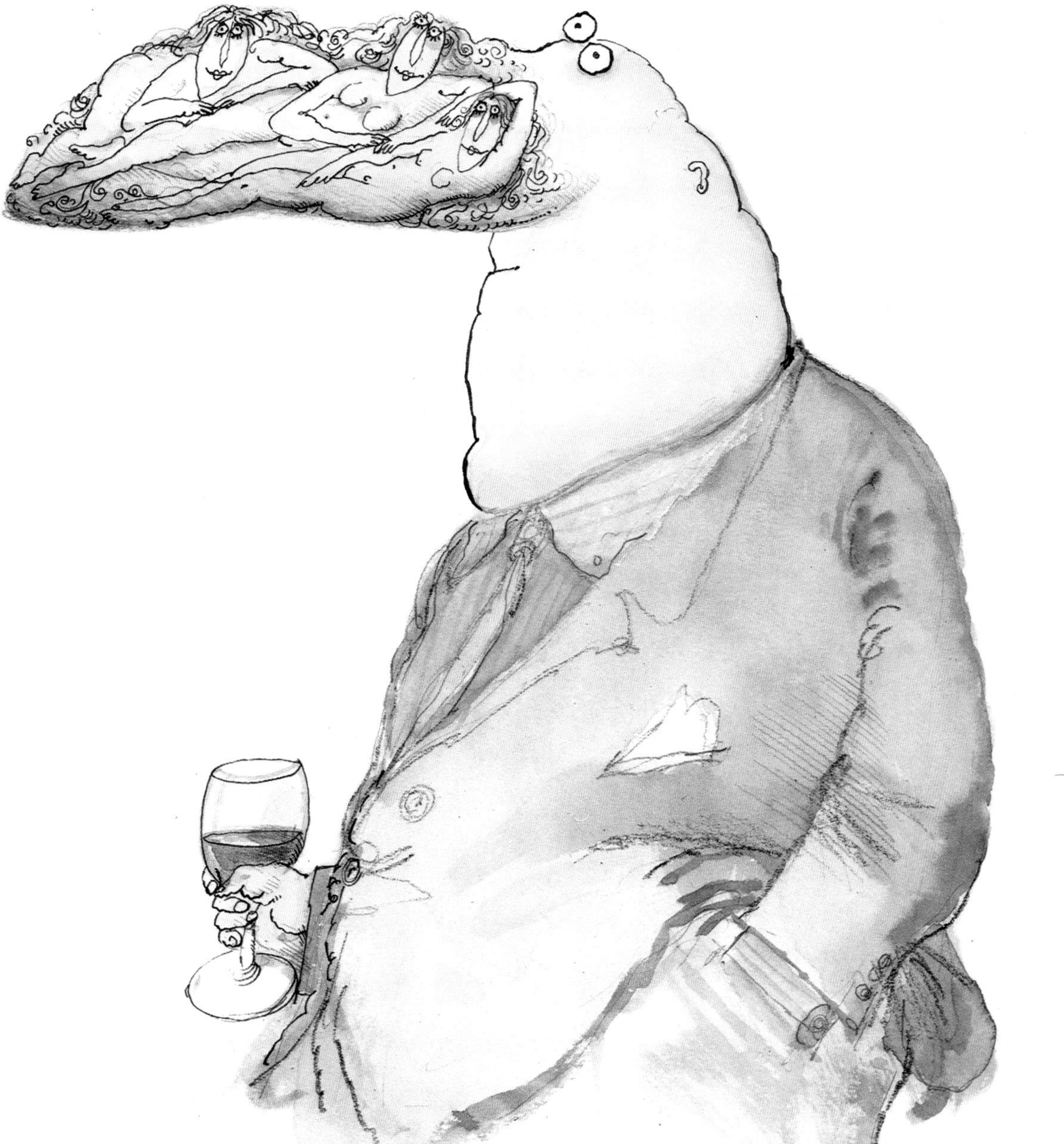

Fullish body, but beginning to fade

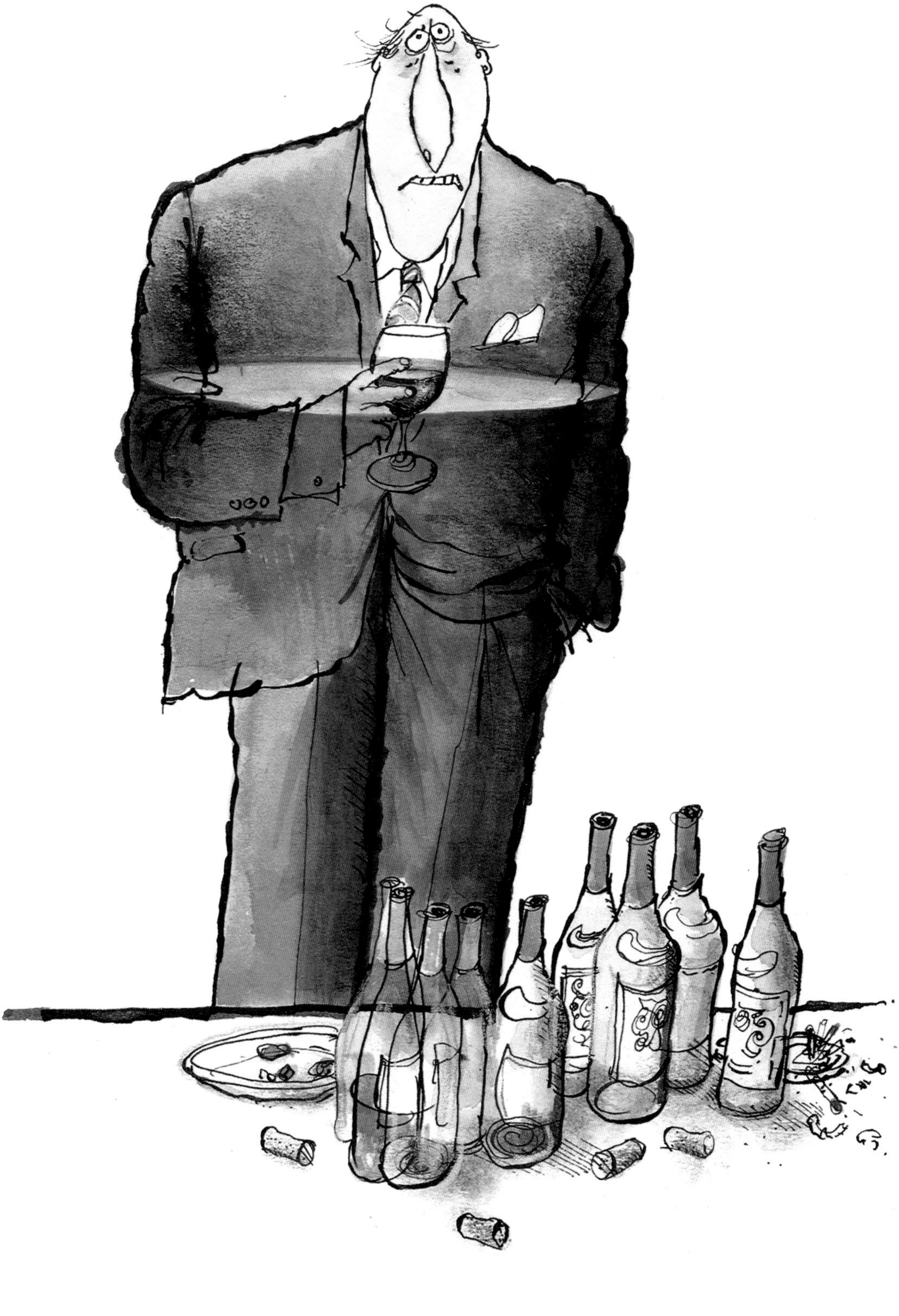

Rather backward

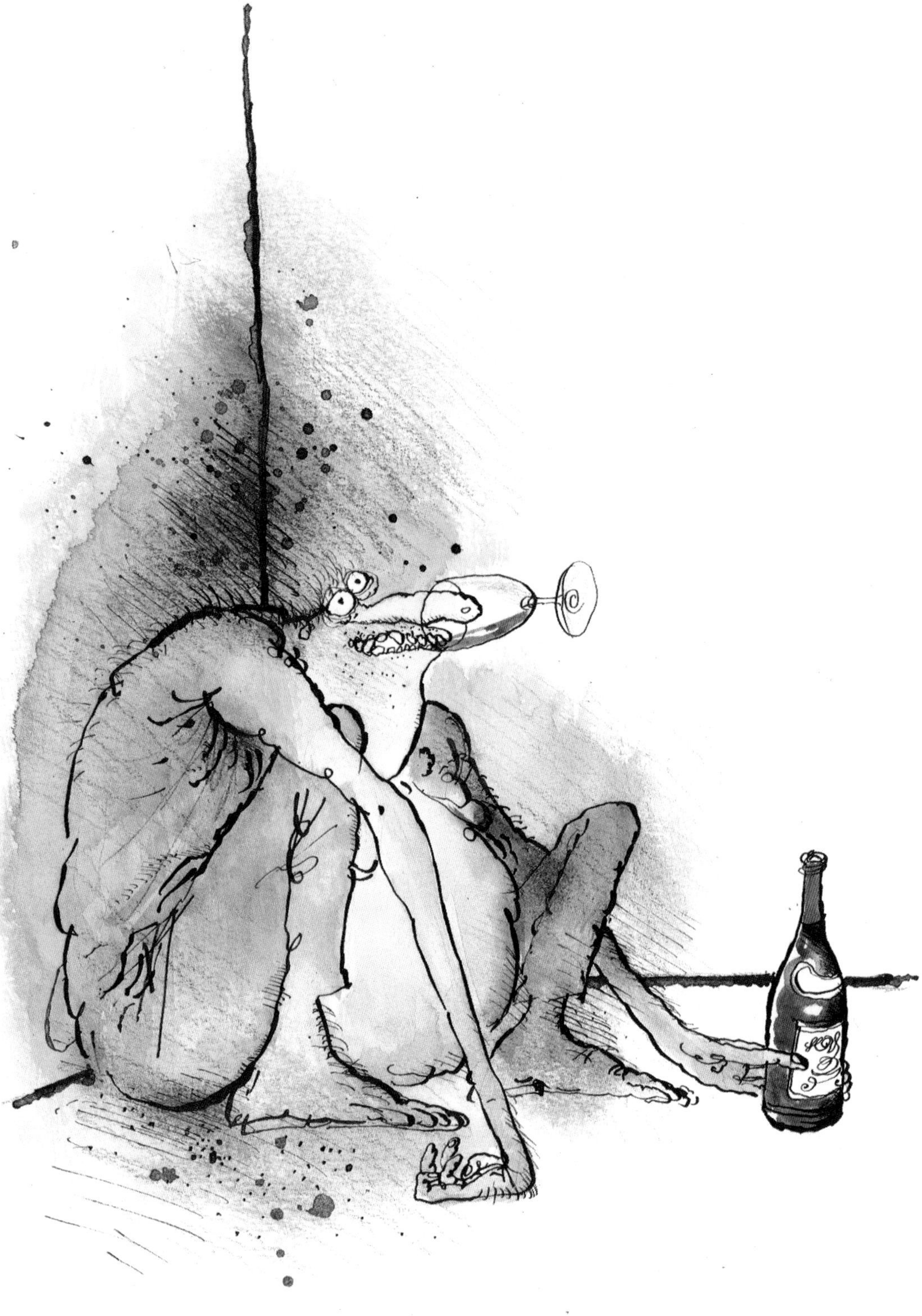

Has voluptuousness and charm

in an earthy sort of way

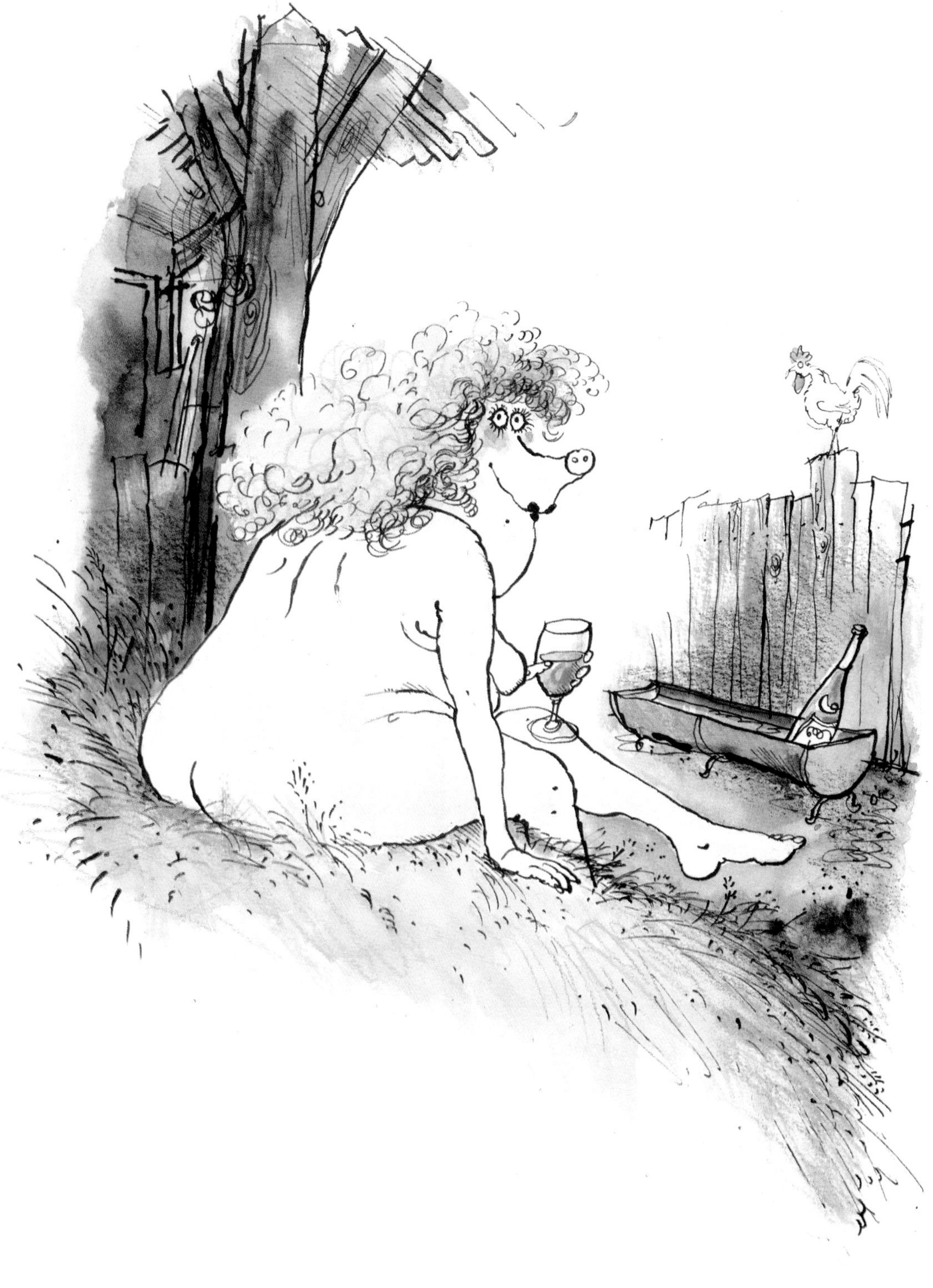

Knit to a harmonious whole

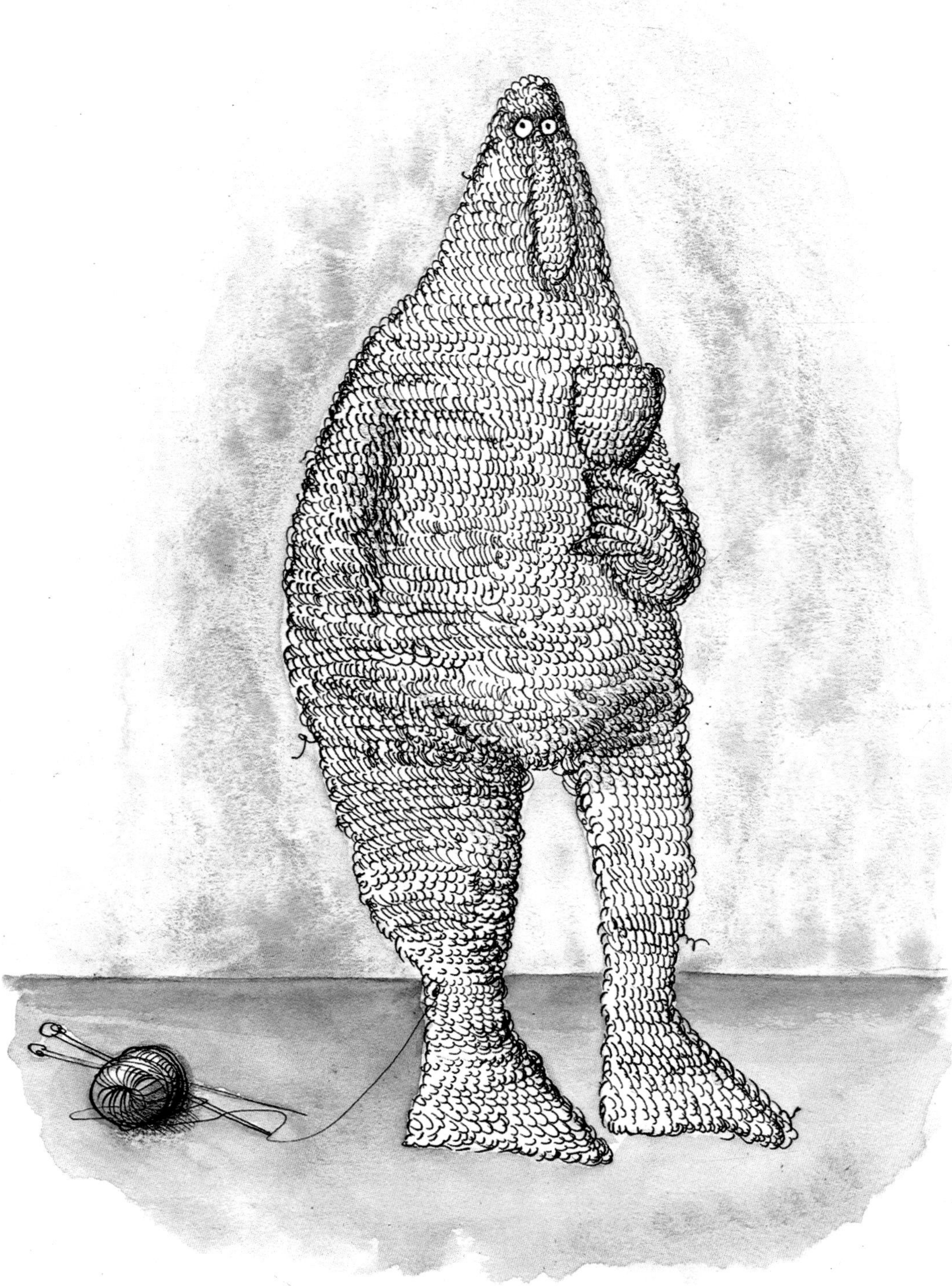

Should remain in the cellar
for two or three years

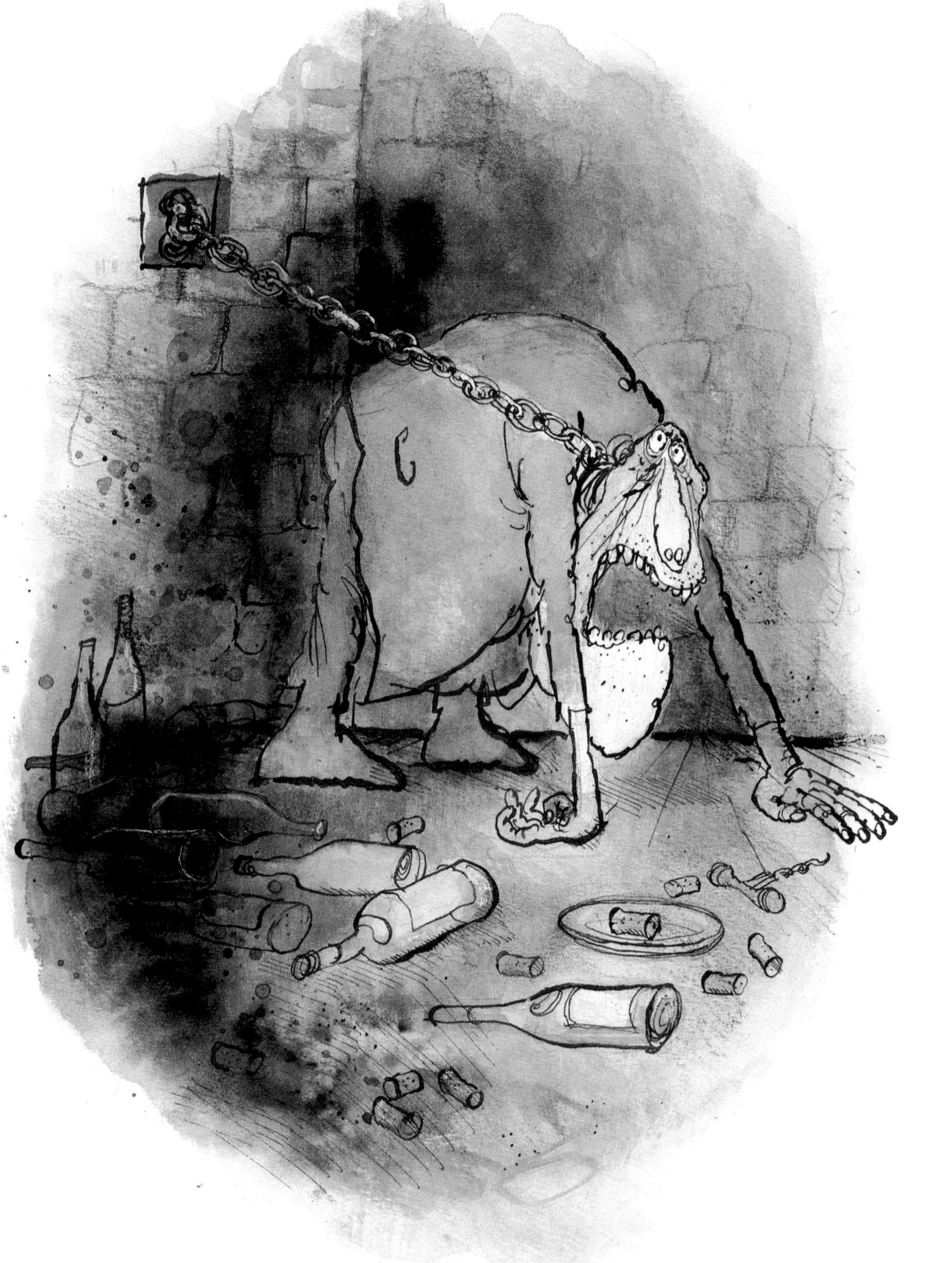

Rather special

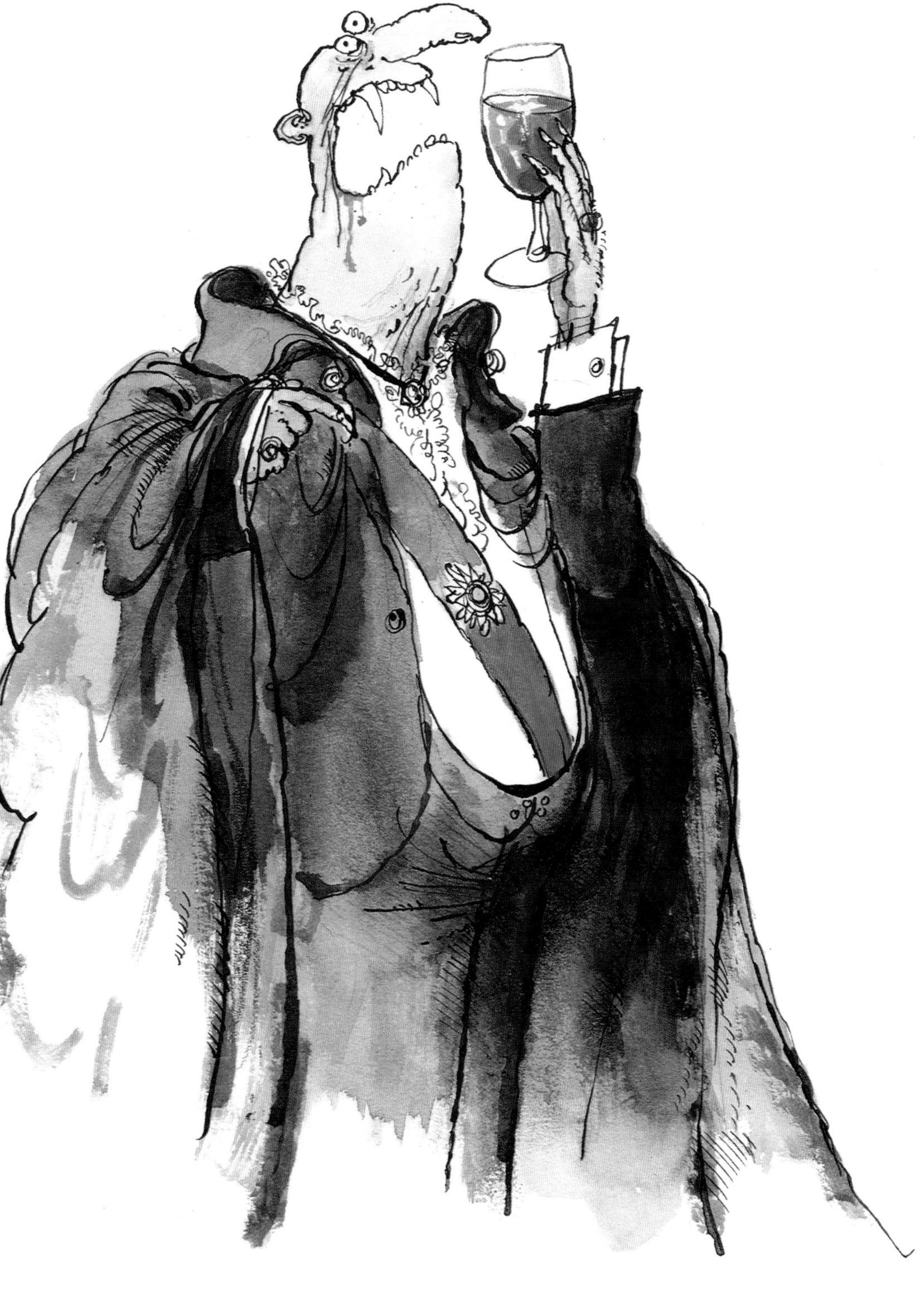

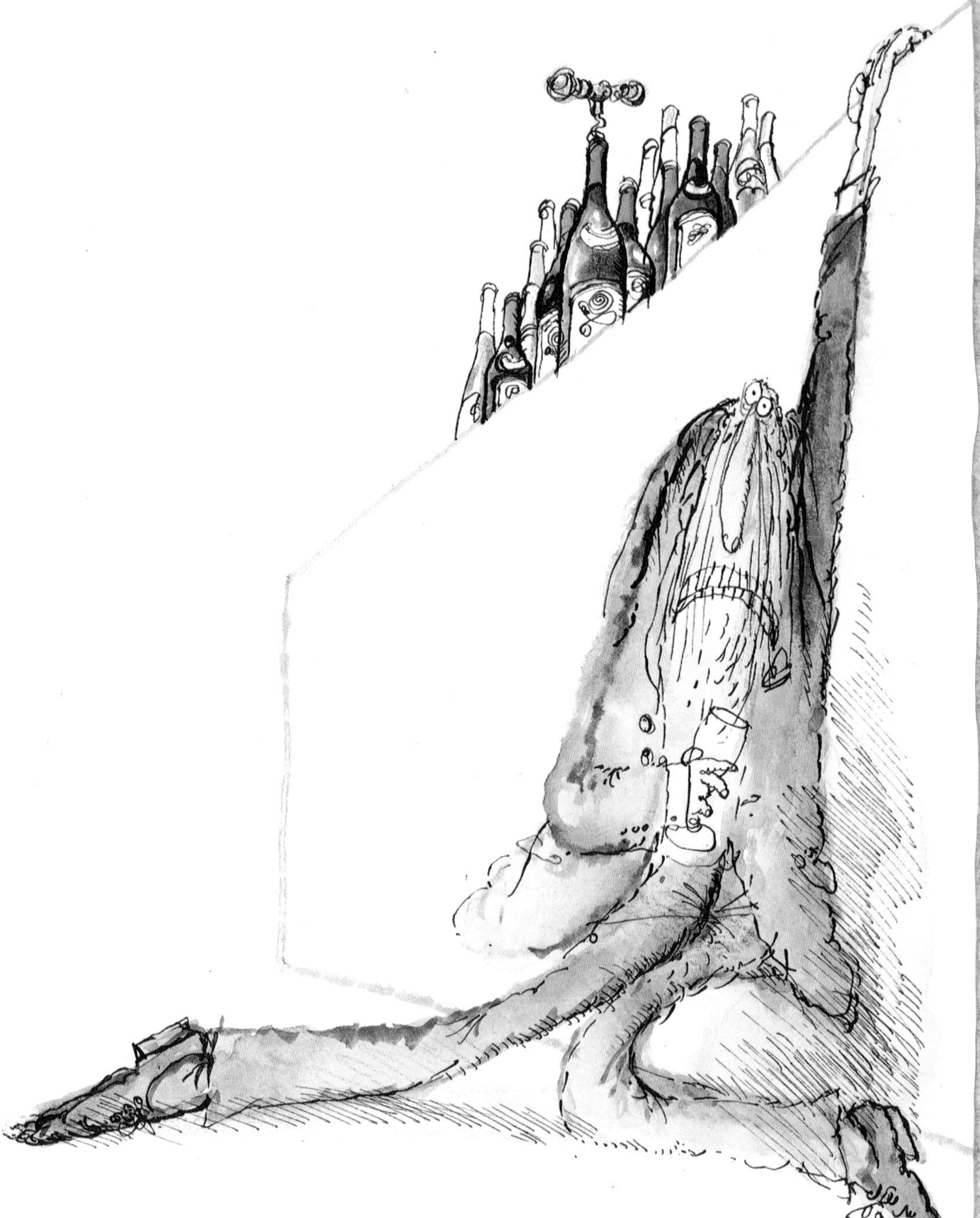